JANEK & JADWIGA

A Heartwarming Story

of Love and Respect

between Mother and Son

By Helen Glowacki

This is a true story as relayed to the author by the subject of the narrative, Jan Puljanowski. It is his story of growing up in Europe as war raged through his homeland and of the mother who taught him how to love despite what the world brought to his doorstep.

The King James Version (KJV) of the Bible, which is public domain in the United States, is used throughout the books by this author. For further study, the author recommends the New King James Version (NKJV) of the Bible as easier reading and less usage of the old world language while remaining true to the original text.

This book was printed in the United States of America.

Cover by: Ghislain Viau, Creative Publishing Book Design, Inc.

To order additional copies of this book visit www.helenglowacki.com or Amazon.com

"But if we hope for that we see not, then do we with patience wait for it."

Romans 8:25

JANEK & JADWIGA

A Heartwarming Story

of Love and Respect

between Mother and Son

By Helen Glowacki

Novels by Helen Glowacki
When God Broke Grandma's Heart
When God Took Grandma Home
When Grandma Chased the Spirits
The Granddaughter and the Monkey Swing
The Story of God's Plan of Salvation
Abiding Faith, Hidden Treasure
And Then They Asked God
Caleb's Testimony
Janek and Jedwigna

Why God Why Series by Helen Glowacki
To What Purpose?
Why God Why?
Why Trust Scripture?
Life after Death And The Coming Tribulation
What Does God Want Me To Do RIGHT NOW?
Do Our Little Sins *Really* Count?
What Do Angels Do?
What is Faith?
Satan's Gift of Fear

Other non-fiction Books by Helen Glowacki
Politically Incorrect: The Get Some Gumption
Handbook When Enough is Enough
Overcoming Depression: How to be Happy
What No One Is Telling You about Addictions
Angels, Aliens & Chariots

****

Authors Websites: www.helenglowacki.com
www,scripturalinsight.org,
Face book: http://www.facebook.com/pages/

MISSION STATEMENT

To Serve
God

With All Our Strength
And

All Our Heart

Helen Glowacki

"One thing have I desired

of the Lord,

that I will seek after;

that I may dwell

in the house of the Lord

all the days of my life,

to behold the beauty of the Lord,

and to enquire in his temple."

Psalm 27: 4

ACKNOWLEDGEMENTS

Special thanks to a very special young lady named "Izzy" who is the greatest cheerleader one could have for this book.

Special thanks to Richard Levinson for providing the first opportunity through which I could develop my writing skills, and to my brothers, sisters and ministers in faith who give so freely of their love and prayers.

And to my Face Book friends who pray for me and support my ministry.

But most of all, my heartfelt, humble thanks to our Heavenly Father for His inspiration, guiding hand, protection, and never-ending love.

May this work bring joy to His heart and help find that last soul!

"And the Spirit, and the bride say,

Come.

And let him that heareth say,

Come,

and let him that is athirst come.

And whosoever will,

let him take the water of life freely."

Revelation 22:17

DEDICATION

This book is dedicated to my wonderful husband

Janek Puljanowski.

It is also dedicated to his sister

Waclawa Puljanowski Paolantonio,

and is a tribute

to their mother Jadwiga Puljanowski.

TABLE OF CONTENTS

Acknowledgements   Page   13

Dedication   Page   11

Table of Contents   Page   15

Chapter 1: 1908 Jadwiga   Page   17

Chapter 2: 1911 Albin   Page   25

Chapter 3: 1935 Jadwiga & Albin   Page   31

Chapter 4: Janek   Page   39

Chapter 5: Waclawa   Page   51

Chapter 6: 1956 A Profession   Page   57

Chapter 7: 1965 America   Page   65

Chapter 8: 1970 English   Page   73

Chapter 9: 1972 Responsibilities   Page   77

Chapter 10: Ethics   Page   81

Chapter 11: Heartbreak   Page   87

Chapter 12: A Life to Celebrate   Page   91

About the Author   Page 101

Synopsis of this Authors Books   Page 103

Book Reviews   Page 108

Description of Novel Characters   Page 117

CHAPTER ONE

1908 JADWIGA

*"The Lord hath appeared of old unto me,
saying Yea, I have loved thee with an everlasting
love:therefore with loving kindness
have I drawn thee."*

Jeremiah 31:3

Jadwiga had such a beautiful singing voice that people passing on the road would stop and listen for a while. She was singing again as she always did when she worked…..and all who heard smiled as they listened. Her family and friends and even strangers who heard her gentle voice seemed comforted by the beauty, elegance and the joy with which she sang. For just a little while in the war-torn country of Poland one could erase the worries they carried day and night as they listened to the soft music. Even as a baby, the sounds she made were a joy to hear.

.

Jadwiga was born on May 17th in 1908 in the town of Wilno, now the capitol of Lithuania. At that time, Wilno was a part of Poland. Her father, Jan Poplawski was 6 foot 2 inches tall and yet she never grew past 5 feet tall. Her mother's name was Victoria.

Famine ruled the land during this period of time and somewhere around 1909 when Jadwiga was nine months old, her father Jan decided to sell all that he had and bring his wife and two children to the United States. Nine million others came to the United States during the famine in Europe. All wanted to escape poverty and starvation and the effects which the war had on their lives and their country..

The Poplawski family prospered in the United States and remained in Boston until 1913 allowing Jadwiga to have a short experience in an American school where she developed the saying "My Golden America". Jadwiga's father Jan had migrated with his family to Boston because he knew that Boston had a large Polish population. Although he also spoke Lithuanian (because they'd lived along the border of both Lithuania and Poland), he felt that the entire family could communicate more easily with others whose native tongue was Polish.

Once in America, Jan did well in his job as a professional baker. He was happy and prospered. The family enjoyed a spacious 12 room apartment, good food, a steady income and an excellent school system for their children. Jan's wife, (Jadwiga's mother Victoria Litaszewska) was also industrious and rented out some of the excess rooms of the large apartment for extra income. She also cooked for her tenants which enabled her to earn even more money to add to the family's savings.

Victoria's efforts and Jan's income as a baker enabled them to live well and to save money which inspired Jan's belief that if he could amass enough money he could go back to Poland, purchase a large section of land and hire tenant farmers to do the work for him. He longed to become a rich landowner in Poland and show everyone what a wise business man he was. Thus began a deep desire see his dream unfold. Times were good and they had all the money they needed.

But when Jan told his boss about his plan to return to Poland, Jans' boss warned him against putting his plan into place, explaining that war was imminent in Europe. He told Jan, that in such a war he could lose everything he'd worked for here in America. He also reminded him that he and his family were safe in the United States and could count of continuing to earn a good salary as a baker. Jan would laugh and reply to this warning with the Polish words: *"Komu wojna to wojna a mnie krowa dojna"*. Translated this meant *"For whom war it is war... but for me it will be milking a cow"*.

In time, Jan's dream of returning to Poland was fulfilled. However, shortly after he arrived back in Poland with the money he'd earned and saved in the United States, war did indeed break out and in due time, Jan Poplawski lost everything he'd earned. He and his family suffered greatly from this loss and he realized what a terrible mistake he'd made. Every day of his remaining life he regretted ever leaving the United States. He often said that if he could...he would crawl across the ocean floor on his knees to return to the United States.

As war spread throughout Europe and everyone struggled to find enough food and proper shelter for their family, Communism gained in strength and the government took possession of everything anyone owned. With Communism no one was allowed to own anything individually. Everything was considered *"community property belonging only to the "state"*. The family starved and their bellies swelled from lack of proper nourishment. Jadwiga's mother Victoria became embittered and began to take out her rage and disappointment on her family. Jadwiga was affected most strongly as she worked side by side with her mother each and every day just so the family could survive. Jadwiga's relationship with her mother became so strained that Jadwiga realized that she needed to learn as much as she could so she would one day be able to go out on her own.

The entire family suffered under the inner anger of her mother but each was so dependent upon the other that they had to remain together. Some family members joked about the knick-name they'd privately selected for Victoria since she had became embittered. They secretly called her "Jedza" which meant "witch" in Polish.

Famine had first hit Poland when World War 1 broke out from 1914-1918. After 1918 Poland was granted its freedom but this ended in 1939 with the start of World War 11 when both Russia and Germany invaded Poland.

Sadly Jadwiga's family returned to Poland just as World War 11 began and a great famine pervaded the land once again. Many fled under the threat of the Russian land grab where landowners unwilling to give their land over to Communist rule were sent to Siberia.

Despite the harsh conditions, Jadwiga still sang everyday as she learned new skills through hard work. With her happy heart and willing nature she adjusted to what circumstances she and her family faced. And though her mother exacted a toll on Jadwiga she did teach her how to knit and crochet, how to cook and how to preserve food. She taught her how to find rare roots and foods in the woods hoping these would help sustain them.

Jadwiga had come into these difficult circumstances when she was very young. After her experience of attending school in the United States she recognized how fortunate she was to have been in the United States to witness firsthand that life could be very different than what she was now experiencing. She always remembered those times when they had plenty of food, when she lived without fear of soldiers, when she had the camaraderie of other children.

Now however, her easy going nature and accepting spirit allowed her to face the reality of what they had to endure. With a strong determination to make everything as good as possible she learned what she could and worked hard. Nevertheless, born into her heart was a desire to someday return to the United States. Jadwiga also learned from the experience and wisdom of her parents…and from the struggles of life in Poland during the war. She learned from the terrible consequences of Communism…..lessons which she would inadvertently pass on to her son. She worked hard to master the art of sewing, knitting and crocheting which was to help her as she began her own family. In time she attended sewing classes to earn extra money as a seamstress.

Jadwiga learned how to shear a sheep, glean the fibers from the wool and make thread. She learned that she could control the thickness of the threads by how she pulled the fiber together and placed it on the spinning wheel. Thus she learned how to create more warmth for her family by making the threads thicker. Jadwiga could make socks, sweaters, coats and other items the family required to ward off the cold. There was no heat, running water, or electricity in the bombed out homes in which they lived and everything she could do to keep everyone warm in the cold of winter was very important and very much appreciated.

Eventually, because Jadwiga and her family were always hungry, they expanded their farming efforts. They managed to grow some food and raise chickens and learned to hide these treasures when the soldiers came. But soldiers would often find what they hid and take everything they could when they were in the area. It became a never ending struggle to feed themselves. After soldiers, the wandering gypsies would also come looking for a chicken to steal.

Continuing to live on the border between Lithuania and Poland, Jadwiga witnessed the conflict between these countries and also the conflict within the church. The church, torn between two countries and two languages was ordered to conduct the early mass in Polish and the later mass in Lithuanian.

For many years a fight for dominance angered the people and the church and the two morning masses.... though held in a different language.... still brought about a great contention. Sometimes the fighting was so intense that the Monsignor would close down the church for weeks as the argument continued. It was in this atmosphere that Jadwiga was taught not only what she needed to know to live, but also what she needed to know to nourish her soul and keep her in God's good graces....but she also learned to speak directly with God for God's help and not trust everything the church said.

Despite this upheaval, Jadwiga never lost her faith and in the future was to raise her children with full knowledge of church doctrine and a love for God, but also with the ability to reason for oneself. Jadwiga never doubted God even though her prayers seemed not to be heard nor even be considered in the heavens. Nevertheless she remained stedfast in her faith. Watching how she dealt with these situations, touched the hearts of her children giving them a lasting impression of a good and faithful God even when they themselves had sometimes given up on God. Just as Jadwiga learned to reason so did her children by her example.

"And the Lord said unto him,
"I have heard your prayer and supplication that
thou hast put before me."

1 Kings 9:3

CHAPTER TWO

1911 ALBIN

"Fathers, provoke not your children to anger,
lest they be discouraged."

Colossians 3:21

Albin was to become Jadwiga's husband. He was born on October 17th in 1911 in the village of Dembina which was 60 km west of Wilno. His father was Josef Puljanowski and his mother was known as Kamila. He had one brother, named Alexander and two sisters named Stasia (Stella) and Helen.

Albin was the youngest child. When he was only about one years old whwn his father left Poland to go to the United States taking his two daughters with him. He planned to send for his wife (Kamila) and baby son Albin as soon as he earned enough money to do so. Alexander, the oldest son had already left home to make his own way in the world. However.....Josef Puljanowski never came back to Poland......and never sent for his wife or son.

As a result of his fathers' abandonment Albin's life was very hard. He and his mother (Kamila) could barely find enough food on which to survive. His mother was always afraid, fully understanding that she was in great danger to be living in a tiny cottage with only her young son and no one to help her. As soldiers swarmed the area, crazed with their war effort, they were often boisterous and cruel.

There were many times when Kamila thought that the soldiers would kill them, especially when she had no food to offer them. They accused her of hiding food even though they could see how thin Kamila and her son looked and could find no evidence of any food in the house or fields.

One day, when the soldiers came again, (this time they were Russian soldiers) and Kamila had no food to give them, their anger went out of control and they decided to rape Kamila to get even with the fact that she had nothing else for them.. They kept her little boy Albin, then about four years old, outside of the house with the soldiers while each waited for their turn with Kamila.

Thus, during World War 1, in 1914, when a band of Russian soldiers swept through the village, confiscated their home and all in it, Albin's mother Kamila, was raped by the entire platoon of soldiers and died as a result. When the soldiers left, Albin found his mother dead and found himself an orphan with no family to care for him. He was only four years old. There wasn't even a friend or neighbor to take him in as all the people could barely feed themselves let alone feed an unrelated child who could not earn his keep.

Though he could not read or write, never having gone to school, at the age of four, Albin spoke three languages: Lithuanian, Polish, and Russian. This allowed him to understand much of what the soldiers said and did. It helped him understand how the people around him viewed his plight and why they did not want to help him.

Albin could not read or write and was not yet strong enough to work the land. There was no one to take him in as food was scarce for all the people. This left Albin totally alone and all he could do was to search for the elusive roots and berries he'd seen in the woods and to sleep in the fields under some hay to keep warm. Once in a while he was allowed to sleep in someone's barn.

Albin was always begging for food and looking for scraps of food others did not want. He begged for food until he was strong enough to work for it. He learned much about life during this difficult time and he became bitter and distrustful. He watched the farmers as they worked so he could learn what they did and how they did it. He watched the craftsmen so he could learn their skills as well. He became more and more determined to grow up quickly and develop every skill he could to enable him to earn his food.

Thus Albin never saw the inside of a classroom and never learned to read or write. But he could work hard and eventually, by watching, he did learn all that was possible about farming and animal care. Sadly, without a family, he was never taught any social graces nor how to express love. His pain was so great at times that he had trouble controlling his anger.

Albin was a hard worker, took any kind of job he could get, was praised by his bosses, and was punctual and reliable. Sometimes however, he had little initiative because of a sense that he was and always would be inferior to those with schooling and special skills. Thus he could be lazy at times, giving up easily and of course, he was too quick to anger.

But, to his credit, Albin had developed good farming skills and some construction skills. He also developed an excellent sense of direction. When in the woods or searching for a special kind of berry or mushroom, he always knew where to look when others could not find what they sought. No matter how deeply imbedded in the woods he was, he always and immediately knew how to get home.

Albin was not religious and did not attend mass except for Christmas and Easter...but he did have a strong moral compass in many areas and conducted his life in a manner which allowed him to meet many standards which the Bible embraced.

This was the man who Jadwiga was to marry and the man who was to become the father of a little boy named Janek who was to emmigrate to the United States and be the success the whole family at one time could only dream of.

But life, in the meanwhile, held many challenges for Albin. After marrying Jadwiga who was three years older than he, he seemed to stop trying to improve, and relied on Jadwiga for everything. He was to recognize the value Jadwiga brought to his life but sadly was unable to express his feelings for her. Maybe he was also unwilling to do so. Since he'd never known love, he could not give love or express love in any way. His lack of desire to face reality, to care about what others needed was to separate him emotionally from his wife and children for the rest of his life...and also separate him from any meaningful relationships.

But something inside him had taught him to respect Jadwiga's dream of one day going to her "Golden America". He therefore never interfered with her desire to bring their family to the United States despite the fact that the slow and difficult pace of his life often made him feel that such a dream was impossible to achieve.

Nevertheless, Albin had been somehow programmed to accept that Jadwiga never gave up. In time he watched and often privately marveled as Jadwiga worked to instill the wonder of her long held dream into their son's heart. He'd smile thinking that no matter how hard her children might kick and scream against moving to another country, they would eventually do as she said!

*"When thou passest through
the waters,
I will be with you and
through the rivers,
they shall not overflow thee"*.

Isaiah 43:2

CHAPTER THREE

ALBIN and JADWIGA

"Be not conformed to this world; but be ye transformed by the renewing of your mind, that ye may prove what is that good and acceptable and perfect will of God."

Romans 12:2

Albin and Jadwiga met in 1933 when Jadwiga was 25 years old and Albin was 22 years old. In those days, Jadwiga was considered an "old maid" for lack of a husband even though she was only 25.

Jadwiga and Albin dated for 2 years before they married. They had to wait longer than they'd planned because when Jadwiga applied to the church for permission to marry, she was told that she would not be issued permission to do so because neither she nor her family had paid their church "taxes". The church would not marry them until the taxes were paid, even though the family didn't even have enough money for food.

Therefore she and Albin had to work extra hours for well over a year just to save enough money to pay "back taxes" to the church so they could obtain permission to marry.

Finally, they were married in January of 1935. But even with all their sacrifice and struggle, their life was still difficult in many ways. The first terrible heartache for Jadwiga in her marriage was that her first child was stillborn, arriving when she was seven months pregnant near the end of 1935.

Jadwiga blamed herself for the death of her child. Her mind told her over and over that *She'd worked too hard, lifted things far too heavy for someone who was pregnant.* She had leaned on her stomach to feed the pigs over a tall fence, and she did not eat properly. The death of this innocent little child always weighed heavily on her heart.

But Albin and Jadwiga continued to work hard and began to see the fruits of their labor. They managed to obtain four hektars of land and on that land built a small two bedroom log cabin for the family and a barn for their animals. They eventually obtained a cow which gave them milk, cream and butter and they purchased a horse which helped Albin as he plowed the fields. They bartered for some geese and chickens which gave them eggs and meat. They also grew many different vegetables both for themselves and for bartering for the items they did not grow. They grew the hay needed for the animals. It was grueling work...... every day..... rain or shine.

Jadwiga and Albin had a full term child on June 24th, 1939 and named him Jan. Jadwiga called the little boy "Janek" which was a nick name for Jan. She adored her son and each and every day she taught him about life and how to deal with the challenges and hardships she knew he too would have to face.

As they weeded and planted, watered and harvested, gathered wood, and cared for the animals, she would quote a myriad of Polish proverbs meant to teach Janek the ways to manage his life.

One which Janek never forgot as it proved to be true so many times during his life was that if he did not do a job correctly the first time, he would only have to do it over again! Another was to watch what words left his mouth. He never forgot his mothers words to "Keep your tongue behind your teeth" so he would not speak harmful words. His mother taught him that words....once uttered....could never be taken back.

Janek could sense his mothers love for him and he could sense the sadness in her heart that she could not give him a better life. He tried to be strong for her so she would not worry about him. But he was just a slim little boy having to work so hard to help with all her chores and he could do no more..

Because of Jadwiga's devotion and teachings, Janek developed the kind of a heart which could recognize the difficulty of how hard she worked to provide for her family. He could see and appreciate what that sacrifice was. He often grieved for his mother's plight in life. Thus he helped his mother every day in all things related to running a farm and providing for a family.

Jadwigas cheerful nature, her lovely singing voice and her godly spirit coupled with her little idioms on life made an impression on Janek's soul. He also saw how forgiving she was and....most of all how she always trusted in God's will.

His love for his mother grew and remained with him all his life....and his respect for her willing heart and happy attitude despite the challenges she faced gave him an understanding of people and an inner wisdom about what God must love in His people.

Janek carried this respect for women with him all the days of his life, and was a joy to behold and a joy to those he loved.

However, Janek also developed an inner anger over his belief that God did not seem to answer his mother's prayers. Seeing what a good and faithful woman she was and watching as she'd share their meager bits of food with the homeless, made him wonder why God did not bestow a better life on his mother.

Where was God, why didn't God do something for her? This was a question which Janek carried all his life and which interfered with him fully accepting what God allowed to happen in the world. It was such a powerful thought, wrought with so much frustration and anger that Janek began to lose his faith in God.

On May 30th, 1943, when Janek was four years old his sister Waclawa Puljanowski was born. Her knick name was Wacia. (Wadja) She and Janek were to remain close throughout their entire life and she too developed the same determination for a better life. She witnessed the determination of both her brother and her mother and it became her mantra as well.

The war ended on May 8th, 1945 so for Waclava, the war was not as strong a factor in her life as it had been for Janek. For Janek, listening to the guns and the bombs, running from the soldiers and listening to the tales the neighbors told of great atrocities was always real and always a worry.

For Waclavia, the timing of her birth made her life much better. She had no memories of them running to the woods to hide from the soldiers when they heard the trucks coming. But she did have to live with the remains of the rubble found throughout the war-torn country.

When the war ended, Communism began to raise its ugly head throughout the country. It demanded that no one would be allowed to personally own anything; that everything belonged to the Communist government for the good of the masses. Those who were considered landowners would have to forfeit all they owned or be sent to Siberia. Jadwiga knew then that they were in jeopardy.

In 1946, after careful consideration of what might happen to them if they stayed where they were, Jadwiga decided that they should flee their home and move deeper into Poland. This would mean that they would have to surrender everything they had worked for. They could take nothing with them other than what they could carry or hope to keep if encountering soldiers. This was difficult to do but it was a matter of life or death to them.

They relocated from Dembina to Lidzbarv Warminski where they found only a bombed out pile of rubble for a home, no piped water. They had no sewer system, and no electricity and certainly no place where they could buy food even if they had the money to do so. They could only hope for a stove or fireplace which would aid them in cooking and in heating the small area in which they would live.

Thus they started over. They gave up everything in exchange for their safety. With heavy hearts and a certain amount of fear they left Dembina. The family would just have to work harder than ever wherever they relocated so they could survive. This meant plowing the fields, planting and harvesting, and searching for jobs through which they could provide some income for them, albeit very little.

They also had to peruse the forest for firewood to sustain them during the harsh winters. And...they hoped to find some wild game which would provide them with some meat.

Eventually they obtained a cow and some chickens and borrowed a horse so they could plow the field and plant their garden. But Albin was bitter. Life was just too difficult for him and he not only felt this disappointment, but acted out his frustration in all he said and did.

While Albin loved and admired Jadwiga in his limited way, his lack of education, his almost non-existent social experiences, and receiving so little love in his early years made it difficult for him to communicate, to show affection and to cope with his insecurities and incompetence.

Additionally, this frustration caused Albin to lose his temper easily. Sometimes he just could not cope with the never ending challenges of life and sadly he would often take his frustrations out on his wife in the form of a fierce anger.

Janek saw all and vowed never to become like his father. Janek also saw that whatever frustrations and disappointments Jadwiga felt she kept to herself. But Janek saw too the despair she often felt and knew that her dream of going to the United States was something he must support for her sake.

However, Janek was to one day wish he did not have to follow his mother's dream.

*"For God shall bring every work
into judgment,
with every secret thing
whether it be good, or whether
it be evil."*

Ecclesiastes 12:14

*"..... do good ......for with such
....God is well pleased."*

Hebrews 13:16

CHAPTER FOUR

1939 JANEK

"....He that overcometh shall not be hurt in the second death." And verse 26: *"And he that overcometh and keepeth my works unto the end, to him will I give power over the nations."*

Revelation 2:11

Janek, a blond, blue-eyed baby boy, was born on June 24th, 1939 in Romaszyszki, Poland. On September 1st of that year, Hitler invaded Poland and World War 11 began. Janek's life was to be one of extreme hardship yet, like his mother, he was generally a thoughtful but happy boy. Little was he to know that when he was 16 years of age he would leave his family for 6 years to learn a profession, meet his military obligations and ready himself for his mothers dream to bring the family to the United States.

For now, and to this day Janek could recall his mother's singing and the beauty in her voice. Her voice comforted him as he looked around at the bombed out area north of the town where they were located. Her voice took the pall off the small abandoned farmhouse they'd finally located and into which they moved their meager belongings.

There was no electricity, no running water, no inside bathroom....just a form of a potbelly stove for heat and cooking. Nevertheless having one another, and his mother's positive attitude and willingness to tackle the hard work gave them hope and made them happy.

Thus Janek grew up in the loving and competent care of a strong woman, and a father in whom he would remain disappointed all his life. He also grew up with Waclawa, a sister who was four years younger than he. Janek called his father "Dad" or...in polish "Tata" and his mother "Ma" or in Polish "Mama".

His Dad always called his mother "Mother"; he never addressed her by her birth name. His sister's nick name was "Wacia" and when she moved to the United States it became "Wallie".

Janek's mother was an incredible gardener, always able to produce enough food so they would not starve. But Janek noticed that his mother worked too hard and was often exhausted. She worked from before the sun rose because the house was freezing cold and she needed to start a fire for when the others rose from their bed. She worked until the moon had already risen high into the sky.

He felt sorry for her but there was nothing he could do, except to pitch in where he could There had just been small ways to help when he was only seven years old . But it gave him an understanding of their life. It taught him what it meant to "give of oneself" to others. It hurt him to see his Mother's swollen belly knowing that it came from lack of proper nourishment.

Despite the hardships of the past and present, Jadwiga remained a hard worker and kept her family's needs always first in her heart. Somehow God had given her a special wisdom far beyond her education and her experience. Often as Jadwiga explained her activities to her young son, he stored this instruction in his memory in admiration for how wise his mother was. He was amazed by what she knew.

When he was seven years old, Janek made a set of skis for himself from the curved end boards of a broken pickle barrel. He used pieces of wire to attach the skis to his boots. He became a proficient skier and skied all of his life, later teaching his children to ski as well. He also learned how to ice skate again using whatever he could find to make himself the skate edges needed to attach to his boots.

One of his favorite stories about his mother was her instructions to him about picking a certain type of mushroom from the forest and instructing him not to eat them. Summer was upon them and they were plagued with flies which buzzed their heads and tried to land on the kitchen table and any food they could find. The flies came every spring into a home with few windows and certainly no screens. So Jadwiga began using her special skills to combat rhe flies.

Jadwiga sent Janek into the woods for mushrooms….a very specific type of mushroom with the name "Muchomor". His mother would boil the mushrooms and spread the boiled liquid on a dish which would attract the flies. As the flies sipped the liquid the flies would die as the liquid was poisonous to them. Window screens and even window glass was a rarity once the invaders had passed through the countryside.

One day Janek saw the cows eating these same mushrooms in the field and ran hysterically home to alert his mother that the cows were going to die. But his mother explained that it was the cooking of the mushrooms which brought out their poison and to eat them raw would not cause the cows to die.

Again Janek was impressed by his mother's wisdom.

They raised chickens when they could and hid them from soldiers and from the gypsies which were always coming through the area in their rickety wagons. The chickens were free range chickens so had to be caught to be hidden. Janek knew that the chickens and the eggs they produced were needed for the family to survive.

Jadwiga also taught Janek how important it was to bring the cows back to the barn every night for milking. Janek hated the half mile hike across the field to round them up. So his mother showed him how to dangle a carrot in front of them to get them to follow him back to the barn and eventually come without him going to them. She told him to whistle or make a certain noise but always the same sound when he gave them bits of the carrot and explained that one day they would associate that sound with the promise of a carrot. She explained that all he would have to do was walk to the barn…. make the usual sound, and they would come running to get the piece of carrot. It worked…. and again Janek marveled at how much knowledge his mother had about so many subjects.

They also had a few geese which Jadwiga was grateful for as the feathers from the geese provided the down she used to make the bed comforters which kept them warm at night. Without the comforters, they would have frozen to death in their sleep.

Jadwiga also made all of the clothing the family needed and had in her younger life studied with a tailor. She became so proficient in sewing that her neighbors hired her to make their clothing. This helped them financially...or at least helped them in the quest to barter for the items they needed and could not purchase.

Jadwiga also became proficient in measuring and then cutting the fabric required for dresses, blouses, shirts, pants and all the items one needed to dress properly. She acquired many customers because of her skill but often was so tired at night trying to complete an order that she would fall asleep on her arm at the sewing table..She worked by the light of the nafta lamp.

Janek remembered too how his mother would warn him not to tease the geese. Initially he hadn't listened to his mother and he did tease them thus they often severely attacked him in return. He hadn't known that the geese were territorial and could and would attack anyone on "their" property using not only their beak but their powerful folded wings.

Running to the house after such a sound beating from one of the geese his mother reminded him that perhaps next time he would listen to her admonitions. Then she taught him how to hold a goose so its wings could do no damage to his small slim little body.   The geese still beat him sometimes when he least expected it!

The water for their garden came from a well near the house and one of the everyday tasks of each family member was to retrieve a bucket of water for each and every plant so the plant would thrive and eventually feed the family. His mothers' eagle eye always knew if Janek had short changed the plants by giving each plant only one liter of water. When caught, which was almost all the time….he had to correct the error of his ways and retrieve more water to do the job properly. They did not own a shoulder harness which would have allowed them to carry the weight of the filled buckets on their shoulders. Without the shoulder harness they had to carry the buckets by the handle which they held in their bare hands. The weight of a filled bucket put tremendous pressure on wrist, elbow and shoulder joints.

But again his mother reminded him that if he did not do a job correctly the first time, he would always have to repeat the work.   He was to remember what his mother said all the days of his life.

Many times when visiting neighbors and celebrating a holiday, Janek would hear his favorite instrument which was that of an accordion. He was fascinated by the sound such an instrument made and by how the artist never even looked at the hand playing the bass notes.

One day, when Janek was just a little boy, his mother saw him sitting with a little stool between his legs making believe that the bench was an accordion. He pretended to be "playing" the stool as if it were an accordion and humming the tune he pretended to be playing.

This touched Jadwiga's heart and she began to long to find a way to obtain an accordion for Janek. But they had no money…and certainly there was no store from which to purchase an accordion even if they did have money. But one day, a friend visited them with their daughter who had with her a beautiful child size bass accordion. They listened for hours as the young girl played for them. Jadwiga told her friend how she wished that she could obtain an accordion for Janek and the friend explained that accordions came in various sizes for young children.

The more musically proficient older children needed a larger accordion, and the musical ability of the adults could be recognized by the number of bass notes as well as the size of the keyboard on the accordion. The bigger the accordion the more bass notes it offered and thus the harder it was to play. The skill level of the player could increase only if the bass notes increased.

The friend told Jadwiga that he still had the beginners accordian from his daughters first lessons and offered it to her at a very low price. Jadwiga jumped at this opportunity and even reduced the cost by bartering her sewing skills for the price of the accordion. Thus......Janek finally had his accordion.

Janek played that accordion for a number of years but then his instructor told him that further improvement was useless with such a small accordion and that he needed a larger one to make any progress. The cost of such an instrument was prohibitive for them and thus Janek had to abandon his dream of learning how to play.... and Jadwiga's heart once again knew great frustration and despair. There was no way they could...or would even try.. to afford a larger accordion for Janek.

Jadwiga's dream continued to live in her heart about getting her family to the United States. Deep inside her soul she knew that they would prosper there and be safer than if they remained in Poland. She spoke often of her heart's desire, warning Janek not to become too attached to what he could gain in Poland but to be readying himself to one day go to America. But Janek moved on with his life and did not think that going to his mother's "Golden America" would ever happen. He knew that Jadwiga's memories in America were of good times, prosperity, safety and plenty of food.

Jadwiga's father Josef was always sorry for the mistake he'd made by moving from the United States back to Poland and into the war. But Jadwiga held onto the dream her father had thrown away and was determined to succeed. Her dream would be realized one day, of this she was certain.

Meanwhile, Jadwiga had a family to raise, to feed, to teach and to ready for a different future. She also had to protect them from the many dangers a war-torn country offered. She was witness to terrible atrocities: babies being bayoneted to death, men from her village being shot, the sound of guns not too far away, fields being planted with mines and people with no legs because they inadvertently stepped on a mine, and German or Russian patrols roaming the town.

Jadwiga always feared that Janek would step on one of the mines as he walked home from school. As Janek's toys became cast off rifles and used bullets, Jadwiga's prayers and God's protection was the only thing between her family living and dying. She knew that Stalin and Hitler had made a pact to divide Poland into two parts, half for Germany and half for Russia thus when soldiers from Germany marched across the land, shortly thereafter, soldiers from Russian came from the opposite direction. Jadwiga lived in fear and by faith.

One day after having to move from yet another home because of the atrocities of some of the soldiers, Jadwiga found an old abandoned farmhouse where they could grow enough food to sustain them. In the pantry of this abandoned home she found bars of what she thought was soap. She was delighted!

She removed the bars of soap from the pantry and laid them on the kitchen table. Shortly thereafter a friend leaned his bicycle against her front door before continuing his journey to town on foot. As he entered the kitchen for a drink of water, he saw the bars laid on the table.

He asked Jadwiga where she'd found them. She told him how happy she was to find soap, a commodity which they almost never had. Her friend and neighbor shook his head in wonder…laughed and carefully explained that they were not bars of soap but bars of explosives.

He explained that she could have killed them all by that error. He searched the pantry again and found the fuses used to ignite the explosive.

He carefully removed these items from the home showing them to Jadwiga so she would recognize them if she ever saw them again. When Janek heard what the neighbor said he felt a chill move over him for he'd never told his parents that he'd exploded one at the lake, skimming it across the water. That explosion had killed a number of fish.

Janek was angry with God and did not view their circumstances as Jadwiga did believing with all her heart that God looked after them and protected them from a larger harm. While Jadwiga's faith moved Janek he just could not bring himself to believe and trust as she did. Her stedfast faith both taught and repelled him..

But Jadwiga never lost her faith. She made sure that Janek learned his catechism and understood how important God was to their lives. She realized that he was struggling to trust God but felt that through her prayers and God's work he would one day come to the beliefs she wanted for him.

Though her prayers were not always answered, she never lost the belief that God held His hand over the family in protection. She believed with all her heart that God had plans for their future. She felt a peace in her heart that one day God would arrange for the whole family to come to the United States, her "Golden America"

"....for blessed
are they
that keep my ways. "

Proverbs 8:32

CHAPTER FIVE

1943 WACLAWA

".....thou hast been faithful over a few things, I will make thee ruler over many things......."

Matthew 25:21

Waclawa was born on May 30th 1943 in Wilno, Poland and at one time, like with Janek's birth certificate, the government changed the record to state that she was Russian rather than Polish. But at a later date they arranged to have the proper records reinstated demonstrating that they were indeed Polish.

Waclawa was a pretty child, and like Janek had blond hair and blue eyes. Both she and Janek in fact had similar eyes with the whites so much whiter than most people. This made the blue really stand out. The whites of their eyes remained as clear as ever even as they aged.

Waclawa was not only talkative and fearless but challenging. Unlike her mother she never let something go but reacted to her circumstances immediately and quite verbally. Her family smiled watching her challenge life without any fear and called her a "little firecracker". She would need that kind of a personality to make her way in life!

Janek watched how his little family interacted and early on concluded that he was more like his mother in that he always waited before making decisions while Waclawa was more like his father in making split second decisions some of which they later regretted.

But Waclawa also grew up with a strong work ethic which was instilled in her by her mother. She learned to sew, and knit and cook, she learned to garden and even to care for animals.

Like Janek, Waclawa knew at an early age that she did not want to grow up to be a farmer…..in fact she wanted to be as far away from farming life as possible. Thus it was both of Jadwiga's children who looked for another profession and another way of life. Farming was just too difficult, too challenging and too unreliable.

Janek left home when he was only 16 years old to pursue a vocation in photography which was his long held dream. He was gone for six years, part of it for his apprenticeship and the other for his military service. When he returned he was ready to begin the life he wanted.

Realizing that Janek was out in the world seeking to hone his skills in a profession other than farming, Waclawa gained an even greater determination to leave farm life as soon as she could.

But she too knew of her mother's dream and determination to bring the family to the United States before either of them reached an age where they would settle in with jobs, homes and families of their own.

Thus they all shared in the quest to register to immigrate and to locate the sponsors necessary to allow them to do so. Waclavia had noted her mother's suffering because of marrying a younger man with no education, no specific skills, no social graces and a temper which was not always controlled.

Thus Waclawa formed her own dreams and her own determinations for her life which was to live a far different life than her mother had lived.

Waclawa set a goal to marry someone "mature", someone who had good life experiences, good interaction with others…..and a profession, and wisdom…. and the ability and desire to care for her.

For now however, the goal was to achieve her mother's dream and get to the United States. Thus they decided to contact the family from her father's side who now lived in the United States.

They learned that their father's father, their grandfather Josef Puljanowski who had been residing in Chicago had been killed a few years earlier. However, his daughters, (Albins two sisters) still resided in the United States. So Jadwiga decided to write to both of her sister-in-laws and ask for their help as sponsors so her family could emigrate to the United States.

Jadwiga was careful to explain that they were not asking for financial help, or a place to live, or even a job, only for the signed documents admitting to their desire to become their sponsor.

Sadly however in the long run neither of Albins sisters agreed and the family remained worried about who they could get to sponsor their immigration to the United States.

But God knew what they needed and when they needed it. At the last moment after the Embassy finally said that they could go….and twenty years had passed since they'd submitted their application Jadwiga found someone to help them by becoming their sponsor.

In time they were to leave Poland on the 10,000 ton freighter The M/S ROMER bound for New York. Each of them were permitted to take clothing and $5.00 in cash…..no other assets. Waclavia still had some commitments she needed to fulfill in Poland so planned to fly to New York as soon these were met.

Janek understood that his main focus had to be on learning English… Waclavia was to help by having met someone who knew of some free English classes being organized which they could both attend. But upon landing in America, they were all able to find work with people who spoke Polish. .

In time, they saved some money and moved from their small rented apartment into a single house which they could rent for almost the same price as the apartment. Jadwiga was excited for them and wanted to learn English along with her children.

But sadly, though she tried so hard, the stress and hard life she'd had in the past had taken its toll on her health and what she learned one day she forgot the next. Nevertheless, it was still a joy to her that she and her entire family were finally in her "Golden America' and her children were making headway toward the life she envisioned for them.

Waclavia was to eventually find the "mature" man she sought, marry and have two successful and lovely children and then to enjoy four beautiful grandchildren.

Jadwiga continued to pray for her children and was grateful…thankful….joyful to know that future generations would be able thrive here in her "Golden America"! Jadwiga was content.

"Pleasant words are
as a honeycomb;
sweet to the soul,
and health to the bones."

Proverbs 16:24

COLOR LABORATORIES

CHAPTER SIX

1956 A PROFESSION

"Lest Satan get an advantage"

2 Corinthians 2:11

The school system in Poland provided an education for children up to the equivalent of the 10th grade. They were then expected to apprentice to someone from whom they could learn a trade or go on to a higher "college" education. A higher formal education however was extremely difficult to obtain and limited to only five hundred Polish residents each year. Those chosen for that level of education were usually limited to those with influence, or those in the government.

Janek already knew what he wanted to do. When he was just a young boy he'd been given an old camera and had been fascinated by what the lens projected. He could focus the camera on only beautiful images, eliminating or blocking out the ugly which surrounded them every day such as the rubble and bombed out areas so prevalent throughout his country. He could use light to enhance his subject matter and shadows to hide whatever was unpleasant in that which he chose to capture. He could control his environment with a camera! Ever since the day he recognized the power of that exercise, he'd wanted to become a photographer.

To do so meant that he would have to find someone willing to take on an apprentice. The custom was that in exchange for room and board, the apprentice would work long hours six days a week for that person and learn the skills he would require while doing so.

Janek had to convince his mother that photography would be a means by which he could eventually support the family. Finally, with his mothers blessing, Janek, when nearing completion of his local schooling, began to look for someone in search of an apprentice in the art of photography. He found someone who owned a studio about sixty miles from his home. He applied for the opportunity as an apprentice and was accepted.

In 1956 in Poland, public transportation was limited which meant that Janek would have to move to the city of Gizycko and stay there until his apprenticeship was complete. Also in those days there were few specialty machines or pre-made chemicals which later entered the photographic field so Janek had to learn photography from the very basics of how to create an image.

This extra step of his learning requirements was to provide Janek with skills few had in the United States and cause his work to be in demand! God was already working on Jadwiga's request for her family!

Janek apprenticed for four years and did not see his family in all that time. Then...no sooner than he'd completed the apprenticeship, he had to enter into his mandatory military service which would keep him away from home for another two years.

Again God was working in their lives and helping Jadwiga realize her dream even though none of them recognized what God was doing in their lives at this time.

Once in the army, Janek was asked what skills he had and when he explained that he'd just completed an apprenticeship as a photographer, some of the officers could hardly hide their joy, explaining that they had recently been talking about their need for such a skill.

So Janek, after some basic training to become a soldier and some special lessons in sharpshooting, became an official army photographer. He was delighted and looked forward to every new assignment.

From the mundane of capturing the likeness of army officials, to the reporting of meetings and marches, Janek was also assigned to capturing for logistic purposes the structures and terrains of potential future military targets. He loved his job, did it well and even made suggestions about his work which were well appreciated.

Janek was growing into a man as he fended for himself away from home. He was also growing in the skills which he would need to be successful whatever came into his life when he completed his military duties.

But Janek was always mindful of his mother's words not to become "involved" with any person, any job, or any girl (especially one who could jeopardize the family's goal of going to the United States). Jadwiga still lived for the day when the embassy would approve their request to emigrate.

Jadwiga's words, her dream, her yearning popped into his mind and heart often during days of great temptation and extraordinary offers for jobs and even for dating. His mother's dream stayed in his heart even though he did not find any enthusiasm for going to America. By now Janek was almost 6 feet tall, slender, very handsome, personable, well-spoken and downright charming.

Because his mother made his clothing, he was always well dressed, right down to the special cuff links his mother had given him many years earlier. The girls chased him. His service friends teased him. He succumbed to outrageous flirting but always held back remembering his mother's words and their commitment to go the United States.

As Janek's mandatory military service time of two years was coming to a conclusion he was offered a wonderful job as a photographer in a police department. But his mother's words lived on in his heart and she advised him not to take such a position reminding him that government officials in a police station may not allow him to leave the country so he reluctantly rejected the job offer. He secretly wished they could stay in Poland.

When finally discharged from his Army duties, Janek arrived at home, and visited all the photographic studios in his area. He took a job with a man for whom he worked for six months. His name was Mr. Friedman.

One day Mr. Friedman came to Janek telling him that a relative in the United States had written to him inviting him to come to the States permanently. Mr. Friedman offered to sell his studio to Janek and Janek jumped at the opportunity to do so. He struggled to make the purchase by using every penny the family had saved....the entire life savings Jadwiga and Albin had accumulated.... plus a loan directly from Mr. Friedman himself.

Jadwiga was still hoping that one day the embassy would call and they could go to the United States. But in the meanwhile, they had to find a good way for them to find work which would enable them to eat; to have a job and a regular income. So, they all agreed, and Janek purchased the studio in February of 1964 and began to build his very own business.

Janek prospered as God again stepped in to bless this family and answer Jadwiga's prayers. Not only did Janek succeed in business but also began to attract friends some of whom were women suitable for Janek to marry. But again, his mother pleaded with him to wait, not to become too encumbered but to trust that God would open the door for them to go to the United States. While Janek argued that he was earning more than

Jadwiga and Albin combined, and did not want to leave, Jadwiga argued that Poland was under Communist rule and could confiscate his studio at any time in his life.

Because Janek had witnessed such occurrences many times in his early life, he knew that his mother's point was an important one. So again, he listened to his mother, enjoyed the company of his friends, went dancing, went to the coffee houses, but was careful not to get emotionally attached to any specific girl.

Janek made the personal decision that he'd wait until the age of 30 before he married. This would give him time to build a business and also fulfill the promise he'd made to his mother.... and if her dream never became a reality she would know he'd tried his best

But then, in 1962 word came from the embassy that they would be granted permission to go to the United States. Jadwiga was ecstatic. Janek was deeply disappointed. Life was about to change drastically, and they still did not have a sponsor.

All avenues to finding a sponsor among their relatives had disappeared and Jadwiga turned again to God to ask Him to help them. God did so in the form of a man they did not know personally named Stanislav Radzikowski who lived in New Jersey and who became Jadwiga's unexpected Godsend. Stanley had been a good friend of the family many years earlier before he emigrated to America. Jadwiga wrote to him and promised to reimburse him for expenses incurred and assured him that they would not ask for anything other than the permission to claim him as their sponsor.

Miracle of miracles, he agreed, and in January of 1965 Jadwiga, Albin and Janek boarded the M/S Romer, a 10,000 ton freighter to go to the United States. Waclawa was to come two months later by plane. They would all live together in a small apartment and all would work hard at any job they could find so they could pay Stanley back and then begin to save some money of their own.

God was still watching over them. They found work where the owners spoke Polish and they were paid the fair wages of a beginner. They had plenty of food and a safe roof over their heads. Jadwiga thanked God over and over again for bringing them to her "Golden America"!

".....thou hast been faithful over a few things,
I will make thee ruler
over many things......"
Matthew 25:21

"When I was a child, I spake as a child,
I understood as a child, I thought as a child,
but when I became a man,
I put away childish things."
1 Corinthians 13:11:

<u>CHAPTER SEVEN</u>

<u>1965 AMERICA</u>

"If a son shall ask bread of any of you that is a father, ill he give a stone.......how much more shall your Heavenly Father give the Holy Spirit to them that ask him?

Luke 11:11-13

The M/S Romer arrived in Boston, Massachusetts instead of New York on February 5th, 1965 because there was a longshoreman strike in New York and no ship was allowed to dock. The Captain of the ship had no choice but to move on to Boston, Massachusetts where he demanded that Janek, Albin and Jadwiga depart the ship.

Janek asked how they were to get to New York when they were unable to speak English, and had only five dollars each in their pockets. The Captain was angry, having troubles of his own, but Janek held his position and eventually the Captain provided transportation from the ship to the bus station and paid for Grayhound bus tickets rom Boston to New York.

The bus trip was uneventful and finally they arrived at the Port Authority bus terminal in New York....and Janek needed to find a rest room. He did not know how to ask anyone for directions to a restroom as he still spoke no English. His current need angered him and like his mother, he made a decision which was to affect his future life. He *would* learn English and would learn it well!

With the help of a stranger, they phoned Stanley Radzikowski to tell him that they arrived and were at the Port Authority Terminal in New York City. Stanley instructed them to stay where they were and wait for him to arrive. He explained having to drive from New Jersey to the Port Authority would take him an hour or two. Janek,

Jadwiga and Albin settled in to wait for his arrival. The plan was that they would lodge with Stanley for about a month while they found jobs and then found an apartment of their own. They would pay Stanley rent and pay for the food he supplied until their plan went into effect and they received their first pay checks. All three of them and Waclavia when she arrived, would work at any job they could find. However, a job would have to be found with someone who spoke Polish.

Janek's first trip to a supermarket was a shock to him. He'd never seen so much food accumulated in one place before, nor made available to anyone who had the money to purchase that food. He was impressed and understood why America was called the land of plenty!

Within two months, Waclawa had arrived from Poland and all four of them were encased in a two bedroom apartment (Jadwiga sharing a bedroom with Waclawa and Janek sharing the other bedroom with his father). They were all working albeit for the smallest wages. But they were here. They were in the United States and they were together. Life could start again for them!

Just as Jadwiga's dream to come to the United States drove her every decision, so did Janek's desire to speak English fluently. It was now that even Janek recognized how powerful a drive he really possessed. He saw the power of his will and the sacrifice he was willing to make to create a better life for all of them. So, Janek signed up for English classes twice a week and diligently applied himself to his lessons. He also purchased a tape recorder and asked anyone he could find to read a paragraph into the recorder so he could follow the words on the paper along with the recoded words. He worked hard and diligently, and as he became acclimated to his new surroundings he began to venture out to make friends. Loving to dance and loving to talk with others, Janek went to cafes on the weekends for coffee and then to the local Polish club where he could meet other young people and converse with them both in English and Polish.

Janek was 27 years old and while his plans for the future seemed so far away, he plowed ahead with determination making his desire to speak English fluently his main goal for the present. His plans were to one day own a business in photography and have a wife and family of his own. Janek's family ties were, had been, and would always remain strong and loyal and he was to always care for those around him. Janek worked long hours to accumulate overtime pay and he looked forward to the weekends when he could go to the Polish club to dance and meet people his age. He did not smoke nor drink so what he spent to enter the club was very little and the camaraderie, exercise and music gave him pleasure. He always dressed beautifully. His mother still made his clothing so everything he wore was meticulously tailored. The cufflinks and tie pin finished off his elegant look.

And…coupled with his blue eyes, blond hair, tall stature and good looks, women were attracted to him. His smile, his self assured attitude and his incredible European manners made him popular with the women and with his employers. Janek thrived at work as he often demonstrated a knowledge of photography greater than that of his employer.

For a year Janek's life was a huge and exhausting learning curve and he finally began to be content about moving to the United States. It did his heart good to know that his mother was happy, except for when the behavior of her husband again faltered. Albin took no interest in making a better life for them nor in improving his skills or his position at work. He remained the same….existing and finding fault with Janek, Waclawa, Jadwiga, his bosses, and everything else around him.

His actions impelled Waclawa to leave home and be on her own or better yet, find that perfect gentleman, older, well positioned in life so she could leave the company of her Father. Janek too wanted to master English and somehow, someway begin a business of his own. By 1970 Janek had managed his finances so well that he could purchase a car. He decided to purchase a new car rather than face the possibility of breakdowns and the expenses of repairs. This enabled him to get to work more easily, even expand his horizons to a second job and work outside the general area of the bus service.

Taking charge of so many situations helped Janek regain his self esteem and self confidence. And he began to trust that his goals would be met if he stuck with his "program" and didn't allow himself to be discouraged. He'd even met some young women at the Polish club and enjoyed watching them maneuvering to dance with him. His self esteem finally returned and he began to realize the wisdom of his mother's goals and realize how well she foresaw what the future held, unlike many other people he knew. He saw too what a very special, gifted and giving woman she was.

Janek often reflected on the sacrifices his mother made for her family and how much she'd trusted God to bring her prayers to fruition. Janek was now prepared to take over the role his Mother had played in his life and thanked her in his heart for preparing him for that responsibility.

"Peace I leave with you,
my peace I give unto you:
not as the world giveth,
give I unto you.
Let not your heart be troubled,
neither let it be afraid."

John 14:27:

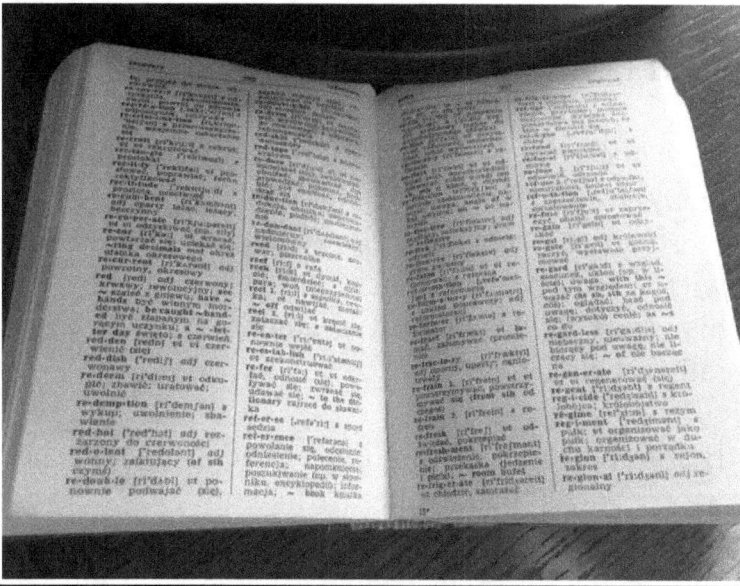

CHAPTER EIGHT

1970 FINDING THE WORDS

".....thou hast been faithful over a few things, I will make thee ruler over many things......."
Matthew 25:21

It was 1970 when Janek began dating and considering when he might marry and how he would bear the financial burden such an action might entail.

His earlier "plans" forbade him to marry as he still had so much to learn and so much to accomplish.

The most pressing job was for him to learn to speak English.

Now however, Janeks vocabulary included so many words that he was often complimented by those around him as to how well he spoke, albeit with a European accent. However, and much to his surprise, his accent seemed to be a benefit rather than a detriment.

But this type of compliment had come the hard way. Janek had worked diligently for years to acquire that vocabulary. He always carried a pad and pencil to jot down words he did not understand. He always had his Polish/English dictionary with him which he used regularly.

He still listened to his recorder to practice speaking and to learn the correct pronunciations, word inflections, and spelling. He'd ask people to read aloud a page of anything handy such as a magazine or newspaper so he could later on listen to how the words were pronounced and follow them on the paper to learn to read properly.

Janek knew that he would one day own a photographic studio. Because of that goal he knew he would have to master the art of reading and writing in English and master an understanding of contracts, documents and sales agreements. His mind was always on the preparations he was making for his future even when he was dancing and speaking with others.

His dream, like his mothers dream was always on his mind and always his goal. Nothing could interfere with those plans. Nothing! It was the driving force in his life during those first years in his new country.

Janek was surprised to learn that so few people had a goal to own and operate their own business. He felt that here in a country where Communism did not threaten to take one's property; there should be more people who desired to learn the inner workings of being successful. Janek did have that interest and that goal because he'd worked toward this achievement all his life....even while in Poland.

Because Janek had actually run his own studio in Poland after purchasing it from his employer, he already had an understanding of the intricacies associated with this type of enterprise and he was anxious to be in that position again.

But he was a practical person always thinking and planning..... just as he did when playing chess. What should be his next move? What would he have to do to win the game?

Therefore Janek dedicated himself first to learning English as impeccably as possible. He wanted to use the language with ease in his associations with future potential customers and with wholesalers and in various legal matters.

To further this goal Janek took a course in the legalities required for a business in the United States so he could learn how to function within the rules, within the laws of the country....their "Golden America". Janek was goal oriented and used to hard work. He'd learned the lesson of doing the job right the first time rather than having to do it over again.

He was driven... very much like his mother was in getting her family to the United States! Now he better understood his mother's tenaciousness in reaching the goal she had for her family. He understood the passion and dream to make a better future for them and began to understand that self-reliance was important to reach those goals.

Day in and day out Janek repetitiously listened to his recorder and made new recordings by reading a page of something he'd found which was of interest. He wrote down any word he heard for which he did not know the meaning and practiced using those words in a sentence.

This practice went on all his life as Janek prided himself on his vocabulary and would often "show off" by using a word someone who was born to the English language might not understand. Two of his favorite "show-off" words were "perspicacious" and "conumdrum".

And as his vocabulary grew so did the list of words he liked to use in public! Yes, he was a bit of a show-off in this respect!

Even later in life, Janek kept a notebook ready for him to add a word or refresh his mind about "yesterday's word". He was always seeking a better understanding of a word or of how to properly pronounce a new word. He never lost his accent but always surprised his listener with the magnitude of the vocabulary he used in his everyday conversations. And, of course it helped that he was someone who loved to talk and loved to be with other people.

Janek was always a gentleman, always gave the impression of an elegant European. He was handsome but felt he looked a bit young for a serious businessman. Thus, in time he grew a short tight beard and mustache which added to the flair and air of Europe which he so easily and yet so unconsciously projected.

Janek would always be grateful to his mother for her patience in reaching her goals and for teaching him how to prioritize his life. Her tenacity and never failing hope impressed him and became a part of his own personality. But most of all he realized that she'd taught him about unconditional love and taught him to be disciplined in everything he did and said. These skills were to last him a lifetime and create a reputation in his private life and his business of which he could be proud.

As his mother watched him prosper and saw the level of integrity with which he lived his life she was grateful to God for how he'd helped her reach her dreams and gave her such a special son..

Janek too felt his mothers peace and wished he could have done more for her. But at least now, in her own golden years she was in her "Golden America" and now she could rest. He vowed to provide her with a safe roof over her head and plenty of food and warmth....and.....to try to give her the peace and love she so deserved. It felt good to know that he could finally do this for her.

These are they which came
out of great tribulation,
and have washed their robes,
and made them white
in the blood of the Lamb."

Revelation 7:14 ....

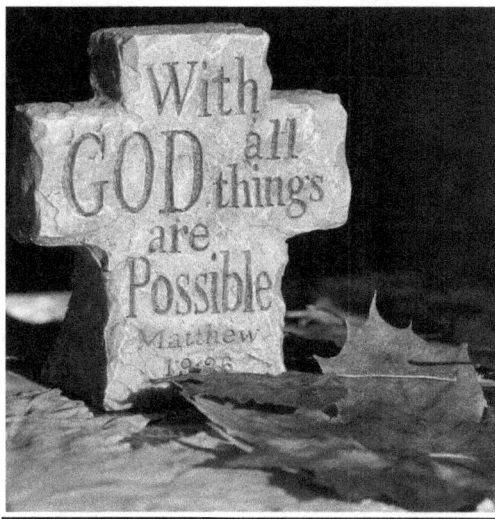

CHAPTER NINE

1972 RESPONSIBILITIES

"When I was a child, I spake as a child, I understood as a child, I thought as a child, but when I became a man, I put away childish things."
1 Corinthians 13:11

Janek launched his own business in 1972 which was to prosper for 30 years. He purchased a building in which to house his photographic laboratory. In that building were two apartments on the upper floor. He placed his mother in one and his father in the other and saw to it that they never had to work again and had all their needs met. At the age of just 34 years old Janek financially and emotionally supported his parents, his in-laws as well as a wife, and two children. Eight people directly benefitted from Janeks hard work, his determination, his generosity and his kind and loyal heart.

Further, in just another few years Janek had the added responsibility of providing work and paychecks to six employees bringing the number of people he had to care for to 14 people! This great responsibility gave him many sleepless nights and caused him to work long hours and many weekends to meet his obligations. His mother's dream and his own dream had come true but was not as easy to perfect as he'd thought!

Janek always double checked the work which left his building to make sure that it was perfect. He worked diligently to gain a good reputation for fine work at a fair price and delivered on time. He was good to his employees, paying a fair wage, encouraging and complimenting their hard work and providing a Christmas party for them each year along with all the food and drinks and gifts such an event would require. Most of his employees also received paid benefits and vacation time. As a result his employees were loyal to him and many stayed in his employ for their entire career.

Jadwiga was content to see her son prosper. Jadwiga knew that God had blessed them abundantly and she was grateful. All her hard work and prayers and hope... and every sacrifice she had made.... had been well worth what she saw happening to her family now.

But for Janek, the work never ended. Luckily he still loved his vocation, but he realized that to run, and constantly expand, a business was a never ending chore to be thoughtfully approached and apprised each and every day. And....technologies were always changing. Machines were being introduced and improved and thus prices were being lowered as machines could do the work in half the time a person could.

Janek had to stay abreast of all the ever changing information and be prepared to constantly upgrade his machines. This meant that he would also have to teach his employees how to operate these machines. Therefore he had to learn himself, had to travel, had to attend seminars, go to various exhibitions, watch what the competition was offering, and keep his work at an excellent level to compete. He also had to advertise and find ways to attract new customers while being sure that old customers were satisfied and would come back.

And it seemed to him that everything had to be done by himself. But again, God was helping him, blessing him with unexpected sources of new business and giving him the determination and strength to keep going.

His financial success was the means through which he could offer many luxuries to his family. However at this point in time Janek, sometimes tired of the battle, forgot to acknowledge that it was not only his own hard work, but the blessing of God which allowed him to be successful. As a result he rarely gave any credit to God. In his heart his good fortune was because of his own hard work and what he had worked to learn.

It seemed as if it were overnight that he was faced with the looming costs of college, of the need for computers, for special tutors, of expenses he'd not realized would come so soon. The machines he required in his business just to keep up were over one hundred thousand dollars each and he'd have to take out a loan to pay for them He'd first have to calculate that doing so would be justified by how much his business would increase.

But again he was blessed with enough business to provide what he required even though it meant working longer hours and even when his heart was not thankful to God for the help he was receiving.

"Put on the whole armour
of God, that ye may be able
to stand against
the wiles of the devil."

Ephesians 6:11.

CHAPTER TEN

1975 ETHICS

".....if ye shall hearken diligently unto My commandments......to love the Lord your God and to serve Him with all your heart and with all your soul..... I will give you the rain of your land in his due season, the first rain and the latter rain, that thou mayest gather in thy corn, and thy wine, and thine oil."

Deuteronomy 11:13-14

Many times in business customers are lost because of their dissatisfaction with the quality of the work they received or the lack of customer service and appreciation with which they were provided.

Janek was fully aware of this and looked for areas where he could improve.

At first he did everything himself...checked everything twice....met customers himself.....and even told his customers that if they were not satisfied, to bring back what they'd received and he would refund their money.

He learned however that many customers themselves were not honest. He experienced one occurrence where a customer took the envelope of completed work in her hand and just ran from the store without paying him for the work. Janek, behind a long counter, knew that to pursue her would do no good. Thus he had to accept the loss incurred by this woman's theft.

Another time Janek had to take a customer to court because the customer claimed that the work was inferior and was the reason he did not pay his bill. But Janek's business and legal skills had taught him to document well and be able to prove that his work was indeed impeccable.

Thus he could produce for the court the signed statement that all work could be returned and re-done if it was not perfect. And....that the work picked up by this customer had been accepted as perfect. Janek won the case and the bill had to be paid.

Janek was always fair. He never skimped on his work, always provided an excellent product and did not mind paying an attorney a fair wage to draw up any papers which would protect both Janek and his customers in the contracts they would enter. In fact, money to Janek was but a means to achieve his goals and never something to be hoarded or worshipped. As others recognized this trait in Janek they realized the strength of his inner set of personal ethics and were impressed. Sometimes they were even intimidated.

Janek was careful to learn the legalities of the country in which he now worked and he tried to do everything "by the book". Janek hired qualified lawyers to help him when needed but often went to court by himself to fight for his own case. He recalls that he went to court approximately nineteen times where he represented himself and he won every case!

Word spread about not only the skills exhibited by Lux Labs, (Janek's photographic laboratory), but also of the high ethics with which the business was run. Word of mouth brought this to the attention of the government, and Janek was offered a huge, lucrative, long term contract which netted him a good profit for many years.

Janek also perfected a method by which he could make enlargements so huge that they were suitable to hang in airports and businesses looking for a means of advertisement which would easily catch the eye. Lux Labs could even produce items which could be back lighted and draw even more attention to the product or business they were to represent. Company CEO's heard of Lux Labs and specifically asked for their services.

Shack O'Neill was one such likeness which Janek placed on these huge boards as an advertisement. But this new technique meant that again, Janek had to provide new technologies, new machines, larger paper, more chemicals, a larger dark room and more skilled personnel to accomplish these miracles of photography! Thus Janek researched and purchased, paid cash and mortgaged to obtain what his business would need to grow and prosper. He seemed to be fearless while at the same time always making sure that his family would not be hurt by any of these expenses. Few people knew of the many sleepless worrisome nights Janek spent trying to carry the weight of his responsibilities alone.

His business acumen was astounding coming from a young man who initially could not even speak English; a young man who came to the United States kicking and screaming about leaving his lab in Poland. Again, the blessing Jadwiga had incurred for her family was still working!

But then came the advent of the cell phone and the technology allowing those phones to take photos and transfer them to computers. No film, no special machinery, no chemicals, no skilled personnel were required to produce the images once limited to being created through a special photographic studio.

This new technology represented the death of businesses for thousands of photographers, laboratories and studios all over the world! And ironically this technology was introduced and instituted by the very business which gave them birth.... such as Eastman Kodak Company.

As Janek realized what was occurring and where this phenomenon would end, he began to think about how he could possibly survive in such an atmosphere.

He told his family that he did not foresee a way in which the laboratory could remain viable and that their only recourse would be to sell his equipment and make plans to retire, albeit years before he'd planned to do so.

He lost money...in fact a lot of money. But again the protection of our Heavenly Father obtained through the faith and never ending prayers of his mother, continued to lead Janek's future. Sadly however, while Janek would be okay, he did not acknowledge that it was his Heavenly Father who protected him. God's help was not what Janek recognized nor requested.

Janek began his plans to retire. While it was a deep, sudden and unexpected blow to him to give up the vocation he loved and the work he'd done for so many years, he realized that there was no other way for him to deal with this new technology.

So again....somewhat kicking and screaming..... Janek changed his plans, knew that his business life had been one of good ethics and great satisfaction and he did his best to move on. What he didn't know was that God had other plans for his future which would prove very different than he'd ever thought possible.

What he would learn ten years down the road was that he would be embarking on a new and different life altogether and through that life he would come back to God.

"Be not conformed to this world;
but be ye transformed
by the renewing of your mind,
that ye may prove what
is that good and acceptable
and perfect will of God."

Romans 12:2,

CHAPTER ELEVEN

HEARTBREAK!

"..... do good ......for with such....
God is well pleased."

Hebrews 13:16

In lieu of the changing nature of photography
Janek made the decision to move to Florida where
he could purchase a new home with no mortgage
and live comfortably on the money earned each
month from a condo investment he'd made many
years earlier. Arrangements for all the clean-up

work required to close a business which represented an entire lifetime of woek, was saddening and aggravating. Janek was unencumbered financially at this point in his life because both his in-laws and his parents had died. Additionally, both his children had begun their own lives and no longer lived at home nor were financially dependent on him..

Nevertheless it was difficult for him to give up a career which had defined him. It took time to adjust to what was to be, but also to find the blessing in it. He often longed for the days when he was back in his lab. He was bored with being "retired". He tried a number of hobbies, he tried some part time jobs, but other than the beautiful weather for which he'd longed all his life, he was not content.

He traveled a lot, ate in restaurants often, and generally lived a quiet, uneventful life. His wife had contracted cancer and died within a year of her diagnosis. Thus Janek, who'd been surrounded by family all his life was suddenly and completely alone. Family had been everything to him and now he was alone with only the four walls to hear him talk.

He visited his children.... sometimes staying as long as a month at a time. He traveled extensively, usually going to Europe on various tours to various countries. While he met other people and had the chance to converse with them...the fact that he was alone ate into his heart and soul. As he reflected on his circumstances, he realized that it was the first time in his life that he was without family; totally alone. It was hard for him to see *any* blessing in the summation of his life. Further, he knew that while he was of a peaceful nature, he was fixed in his ways and would probably not be at ease with any drastic changes. He became heavily depressed as he looked at the four walls which never answered back.

Janek did not realize that God was still working in his life or that God was finding a way to provide him with everything his mother would want for him. Here he was in the warm climate he'd always longed for, in a lovely home with no mortgage, retired and managing well in the financial arena and he was not content. Here he was with grown children doing well on their own, with grandchildren happy and in happy homes and he was not content.

He played his accordion remembering that it was not so long ago that he'd finally been able to purchase a real accordion of his own. He practiced and learned to play by ear. He did well enough and realized that had he been able to obtain the lessons he'd longed for when he was young…and had the right accordion on which to practice, he might have made a decent musical artist. For a moment this thought made him acknowledge that he had indeed been given a good life. But this fleeting thought was not enough and he slipped back into a bitterness which reminded him of war and bombed buildings and his mother's tortured life. He didn't realize how bitter his thoughts were but he did realize that he didn't believe in the God his mother believed in.

In time, he joined an internet dating service and spent hours on the computer sifting through the pictures they offered. He read many of the accompanying biographies. But nothing, no one, stirred his interest.... and looking at the photos made him even more depressed. Finally his organized nature led him to a few photos of people he deemed "pretty" or whose information seemed intriguing. He went on a few dates, but he never clicked with anyone and wondered why he was even borhering. Life was over for him and he should just accept it.

Thus Janek's heartache and belief that God died when his mother had died, made him angry. He tried to accept that he would always be alone. But little did he know that God was not done with him. Jadwiga's prayers had not yet been fully fulfilled.

"If a son shall ask bread
of any of you that is a father,
will he give a stone.......
how much more shall your
Heavenly Father
give the Holy Spirit
to them that ask him?"
Luke 11:11-13

CHAPTER TWELVE

2015 A LIFE TO CELEBRATE

*"For God shall bring every work into judgment,
with every secret thing whether it be good,
or whether it be evil."*

Ecclesiastes 12:14

It was January 2014 and Janek was sitting alone in his too-big and very empty house. He went to his computer to play chess and to see if there was anyone new listed in one of the dating services he'd joined on the Internet. He thought of his life and wondered what he'd have done if he'd known where his life would lead him. He wondered about his mother and how different it might have been had she been able to stay in America when she was young. He'd admired his mother and saw in her what he'd always wanted in his own wife...and hadn't had.

Sometimes such thoughts made him feel disloyal...but it was the truth. Maybe these moments of reflection were to help him see things as they were or to be more thankful for what he'd been given. Maybe his cynicism was because he hadn't gone to church after he left the influence of his Mother, because he'd become bitter with the hypocrisy of the church and those who claimed to be "religious". He saw so many people exhibiting cruelty to one another and religious leaders promising God's favor in exchange for money. His mind wandered and he began ti wonder what he really wanted in a woman...was it just good looks? Was it a calm attitude? Was it the desire for peace or happiness, or maybe even the wish to never argue? Was it the same gentle nature of his mother?

He didn't know the answer and that bothered him. Sure he could check every box he'd listed but would any of that had made a difference? Or could it have been that he didn't have what it took to make someone happy. Arrogant or not he answered his own question with a resounding "Yes, he did feel he could make someone happy". But still he could not seem to pinpoint what he was looking for and now, of course, it was too late for him. He should have been more careful when he was young.. His thoughts were the sad reflections of an old man whose life was coming to an end. But his mind would not stop working, Question after question flowed into his head disturbing him day and night. Had his life mattered to anyone? Had it helped his mother after all? Did his children realize what he had been through; what he had sacrificed for them? Did they know how alone he'd been while living with their mother for 47 years and remaining totally devoted to her and his family all that time? Did they even care?

He wondered if they would understand if they did know his private thoughts. Could he even articulate those thoughts if he had the courage to explain them? Would they understand if he did? And why didn't they *make* time for him now that he was so alone? The truth was that he felt a deep disappointment in their behavior. He did understand the demands on them although he also realized they'd never had to suffer as he did. He tried to overlook his disappointment. As his mind wandered and he leafed through the hundreds of photos of women looking for men on his Internet dating service, he suddenly spotted one which caught his attention and back tracked to find it again. In his deep reflection, his disinterest and hurry through the photos had made him to automatically discard them before any actually registered with his brain. He back tracked and found it.

She was very pretty. She looked kind and sweet but surely the photo had been re-touched...she could not possibly be that age and look like that. So he read what she wrote and found it a lot to absorb. She didn't smoke or drink. She was a strong and unswerving conservative. She didn't want any pets at this point in her life. Her kids, like his were grown and gone. She wasn't interested in a shallow relationship and she was smart. He could read that between the lines as what she posted on the dating site was elegantly phrased. But there was one problem that he could see: she was "religious". That would not be for him! But.....well maybe.... he should consider writing to her after all.

He looked in the mirror and saw an old man, wrinkled, unsmiling, morose, defeated, with an uninterested demeanor, and certainly not "a catch" as they say. But somehow her photo drew him and he wanted to see if the picture fit the person. So with what he considered his limited writing skills, he dared to send her a message briefly telling her that he'd read her biography and thought she was a very interesting person. He told her that he'd like to meet her for lunch or dinner at whatever place she chose. She responded negatively, telling him that she could not commit at this time because she'd just met someone else on the Internet and wanted to wait and see what happened. Janek was surprised at the depth of his disappointment, in fact it shocked him. But, stoic as always, he moved on, keeping her photo aside, hoping that circumstances might change. Again his thoughts and his depression and his questions came to his mind and began to overwhelm him with lethargy.

However, circumstances did change and within a week she wrote back accepting his invitation stating that it would be for lunch at Seasons 52 in two days. His heart flipped and he excitedly made plans. He had his hair cut and had his beard and mustache trimmed. He filed and buffed his nails and of course he got out the cuff links to match his tie pin and dressed to the nines in a suit and vest. He was smiling for the first time in a long time. He'd called his sister in South Carolina to tell her of his impending "date". He told her how pretty this woman was despite his being sure that her photo had been re-touched! His sister made him promise to phone her when he got back home after his date to give her "all the news"!

She *was* smart and very articulate. She was as pretty as her picture and she was a strong but gentle person. He was impressed. He was also a bit intimidated wondering how he would look in her eyes. They had a great conversation talking politics, the state of the world, their travels, the gift of friendship, and......to his consternation......the importance of God and a working knowledge of God's plan for the salvation of His children. They did not yet exchange their proper names...she being known as "Christian Quest" on the

Internet.....and they did not exchange an address or phone number except to note in which town they resided. She was in Lake Park and he in Royal Palm which were about a 30 minute drive from one another...which was perfect! He liked her and hoped to see her again. After all, he thought, anyone could put their best foot forward once and he wanted to know if she could do it again! But had she liked *him*? Did she want to see him again? They did see one another again, at a less fancy restaurant located quite close to her home. He dressed just as nicely but without the suit jacket! Again their conversation went well and was easy. They found even more topics which they had in common. On their third date she invited him to pick her up at her home and upon walking through the door, he was shocked by the high quality and fullness of her rather elegant and baroque furnishings. It was beautiful to most people but to him....a contemporary minimalist.....it was too crowded. They'd found their first difference and for her this was a big setback as her home was her castle....and she liked it just as it was!!!! Janek, sensitive to others feelings decided to be careful about any denigrating remarks in the future. He did not want to lose her.

Janek told his sister all about her and also told his friend who warned him not to be negative. Thus he was doubly careful not to say anything detrimental about her furnishings again. Janek liked her so much that he remained very careful in word and deed. He did not want her to find fault in him. She was fascinating and incredibly beautiful! But best of all she was kind, gentle, smart and amazingly accomplished. They dated a few more times when she told him that he seemed somewhat serious about her and that if this was the case there was something he needed to know. He panicked for a moment and listened carefully. She went on to tell him that she was, as he'd rightfully noted, a very religious person, putting God first in everything in her life. Therefore she went to church every Sunday and did not want to date anyone seriously unless he would also attend church every Sunday...with her. Janek was thrilled that she mentioned him in terms of a "serious" relationship and jumped at the chance to please her saying *"Yes, I will be glad to go to church with you every Sunday"*!

He learned that her name was Helen and he immediately began to think of her as "Helenka". She had no idea what a great change it was for Janek to go to church. She didn't know how badly he wanted this relationship work. She had no idea how lonely he had been or how hurt he'd been in the past. But, from that day forward they dated regularly. They found more and more in common and learned that they were indeed very compatible in life styles. They both took their names off the dating sites and became inseparable. Janek brought Helen to meet his friends and they too thought that he'd made a great catch! Helen took Janek to her friends' homes and to the fellowships held at the church. Everyone said that they made a beautiful couple. Janek brought Helen to meet his sister and they too got along very well. Janek met Helen's children and they too approved of him. Eventually they talked about marriage but realized the legal hassle involved and considered not marrying. But then Helen thought about the impact of that decision on her religious beliefs and on the impression they would be making on their grandchildren and they decided to marry after all.

At first Janek did not want to tell his children that he would be re-marrying. He believed that they would be upset and think mainly about the jeopardy to their inheritance his marriage might mean to them. He wondered if even the fact that he and Helen had already decided to create a pre-nuptial agreement assuring their children of their separate and personal inheritance would matter to them. Something inside him told him they did not want him to remarry at all. Therefore Janek simply did not tell his children he was going to and then did remarry.

Helen and Janek were married on August,18th, 2015. Helen assumed that Janek had told his children of their marriage and was dismayed when she learned that he hadn't done so. A hurricane had been predicted a few days earlier and the airports were closed so Helen's children could not attend the wedding. The hurricane took a different path and the wedding and reception went on as planned with Helen's friends and church members and

Janeks friends in attendance. By June, Janek's house had sold and they began their life as a married couple residing in Helen's house. They were very happy. Janek felt...and told Helen.... that he'd never been happier in his life! He now called her "Helenka" the Polish version of "Helen". Finally, Janek decided to write to his children to explain why he'd decided to marry. When he showed Helen the letter, it brought tears to her eyes as it spoke to the unhappiness he'd suffered most of his life. It also spoke of the joy his children and his work had brought him. He admitted that for the first time in his life he was truly in love and truly in total admiration of Helenka's kind and gentle heart. When Janeks son received the letter and phoned his Dad, he admitted that he too had cried knowing that what Janek said was true and must have been hard for him to write. Janek was grateful for his son's response, his soft heart and best wishes. He touched Helen's heart when he called her "MOM"!

As Janek attended church with Helen he began to understand what God wanted from him and how incredibly carefully and lovingly God had looked after him. As he listened to the prayers Helen offered up each night, aloud before they went to sleep, he was reminded of his mother and marveled that both his mother and his wife were such good women and beloved of God. He began to accept that God brought him to this point in his life because of his mother's prayers for him. Janek did not yet realize that it was now time for him to give back to God the loyalty God had given him. Janek knew God wanted him to look after Helen as Janek's mother had looked after him! As Helen saw the changes in Janek....his joy, his opening up to easy laughter, his better sleeping and eating habits, his easy affection toward her... she was touched and loved Janek in an even deeper fashion. He was now sharing her faith, and finally fulfilling the dream his mother always had for him. He often told others that he was truly happy for the first time in his life. He was open to learning and understood that now was the culmination of God's promise to Jadwiga. It was now Janeks duty to accept what he was offered.

This narration is a story of the love between mother and son and her never ending prayers for her family. It is the story of a son's total devotion to his mother and God's reward for that devotion. But it is also the story of the love between a husband and a wife who share God's love and cherish the gift God gave them of one another. It is a reminder that our love is but a reflection of God's love and of God's blessing.

".....if ye shall hearken diligently unto My commandments......to love the Lord your God and to serve Him with all your heart and with all your soul....I will give you the rain of your land in his due season, the first rain and the latter rain, that thou mayest gather in thy corn, and thy wine, and thine oil."
Deuteronomy 11:13-14:

About The Author

Helen Glowacki is an interior designer, writer, teacher, and motivational speaker. She was the host, writer, and producer of the television series "The Contemporary Woman", broadcast by UA Columbia Cablevision. Her writing credentials include an extensive background as a freelance feature and staff writer for four newspapers and for various newsletters and magazines.

A graduate of William Paterson University, Helen received a Bachelor of Arts degree, magna cum laude, in Communications. She also received an Associate of Science degree with honors and is a registered nurse.

Helen donates her books to cancer centers, drug rehabilitation centers, and prisons. She also donates them to the mission schools of *The Henwood Foundation* to use her gift for writing to help others find the love and comforting presence of God. Helen gladly sends her books and brochures to those who wish to help her bring testimony to others. Helen has written a number of well received Christian articles which are filled with insight about scripture and how God wants us to conduct our lives. She posts many of these on Face Book and on her website

Those who have provided reviews of Helen's books tout the beautiful stories in her novels and her non-fiction books as spiritually uplifting and biblically correct. Her greatest joys are her husband, two children, four grandchildren, and time spent in her faith and in fellowship.

For more information:

Visit the author's website at: www.helenglowacki.com and www.scripturalinsight.org. or visit Amazon.com. You can also email the author at: wally_helen@ yahoo.com.

NOVELS
By Helen Glowacki (Book Size 6 x 9)

When God Broke Grandma's Heart: (208 pages) Rising from sorrow to become a beacon of faith Grandma struggles in an abusive marriage until God moves her from unequally yoked and broken to the healing of His love and forgiveness. Her granddaughter Sarah learns where to find answers to her problems and carries that legacy to those she loves. Paperback: ISBN 978-0-9847-2110-8

When God Took Grandma Home: (260 pages) About the heartache of drug addiction, of the enemy who destroys children through drugs, why God allows righteous anger, why we should pray for those in eternity and a description an incredible experience of faith for Matt and Sarah about why God allowed such heartache to occur. Paperback: ISBN 978-0-49847-2111-5

When Grandma Chased the Spirits: (208 Pages) The magnetism of idolatry, it's invisible power, and the heartache of bearing a child out of wedlock brings debilitating panic attacks to Mary and affects her husband Kevin. When Matt and Sarah tell them about their faith, God engineers a miracle to solve what that they thought impossible to resolve. Paperback: ISBN 978-0-9847-2112-2

The Granddaughter and the Monkey Swing: (284 pages) A wedding, a broken engagement, renovating and decorating a home through Divine Proportion, the truth about Halloween, and the gift of role models create a tender story of friendship. Helping through the planning and problems of a wedding culminates in the unveiling of a secret. Paperback: ISBN 978-0- 9847-2113-9

__Grandma's Little Book of Poetry: The Story of God's Plan of Salvation__: (277 pages) This beautiful whimsical story for all ages, begins when Sarah finds a manuscript in Grandma's desk and recognizes the story Grandma read to her and Josh and Caleb when they were children. Angels watch the inhabitants below them struggle to find God. Paperback: ISBN 978-0-9847-2114-6

__Abiding Faith, Hidden Treasure__: (262 pages) Serving in Iraq, Jim loses his faith to see a loving God allow so much heartache. Barbara invites him to dinner where Grandma shows him why creation and evolution co-exist and God's enemy creates the injustices Jim blames on God. Letters from the grave bring an incredible experience of faith. Paperback: ISBN 978-0-9847-2115-3

__And Then They Asked God__: (295 Pages) When Rebecca and Jayden arrive at their college campus they are overwhelmed by betrayal. Losing the values Rebecca once cherished fills her with guilt so monumental that she cannot forgive herself. Chaldeth the evil angel is defeated when God's grace frees Jayden and brings Rebecca's recovery. Paperback: ISBN 978-0-9847-2116-7

Caleb's Testimony: (262 pages) Caleb would have taken bets on his ability to trust God explicitly....until his accident.. Now, he and Ann must face the wrath of Satan aimed at causing them to blame God for their misfortune. Paperback: ISBN 978-0-9847-2119-1.

Why God Why Mini-Series
by Helen Glowacki   (Book Size 5 ½ x 8)

To What Purpose?: (126 pages) This first book in the *Why God Why* series answers questions about why we are here, what we need to learn, and what God plans for us. It is an excellent book for testimony and one you will share with others. Paperback: ISBN 978-1-4507-7580-9

Why God, Why?: (126 pages) This second book in the *Why God Why* Series describes why we experience heartache, its purpose, and how to face it. It answers questions about God's plan for us and what we need to do to be found worthy. Paperback: ISBN 978-1-4507-7581-6

Why Trust Scripture?: (126 pages) This third book in the *Why God, Why* Series addresses the challenges against scripture, who wrote the Bible, the importance of the sacraments, what role Satan plays, and how health and the Bible are related. Paperback: ISBN 978-1-4507-7582-3

What Should I Know about Life after Death and the Coming Tribulation?: (126 pages) What occurs following death, what will happen during the tribulation, and what the seven seals could mean to us are explained in this fourth book of the series.
Paperback: ISBN 978-1-4507-7583-0

What Does God Want Me to do Right Now?: (126 pages) A concise explanation of what God asks of us, how we can live up to His expectations what is required to become a part of the Bride of Christ, and what God plans for the future with or without us.
Paperback: ISBN 978-1 4507-9076-5

Do The Little Sins Really Count? (126 pages) Most of us believe that the little sins don't really matter but scripture explains why they do.
Paperback: ISBN: 978-0-9847-2117-7

Non-Fiction Books
By Helen Glowacki (Book Size 5 ½ x 8 ½)

Politically Incorrect: The Get Some Gumption Handbook For When Enough is Enough: (406 pages) Fifty timely and controversial issues are examined under the politically correct approach and compared to what scripture tells us is the approach that God wants His children to take.
Paperback: ISBN 978-1-4507-9074-1

Overcoming Depression: How To Be Happy:
(258 pages) We all face heartache, and all feel sad from time to time. But depression lingers and can result from many different causes. It can rob us of hope and destroy our relationship with God. Thus our Heavenly Father tells us through scripture how we can tap into His blessing and His direction and brings joy out of tribulation.
Paperback: ISBN 978-1-4507-9077-2

What No One Tells You About Addictions: (216 pages) Discussing the merits of tough love, the selfish co-dependency of the enabler, what scripture tells us about spiritual warfare and invasion, and generational sin, make this book a must read.
Paperback: ISBN 978-1- 4507--9075-8

Angels, Aliens & Chariots (262 pages)
This book is an eye opener exploring the diversity of God's Creation and His universe. It warns that we might be very surprised to learn that UFO's could be the "Chariots" described by the Bible and that there are three levels of heaven. It describes the nine different types of angels and their very specific duties.
Paperback: ISBN 978-0-9893807-9-9

Book Reviews

Reverend (District Apostle Ret.) Richard C. Freund, President of The New Apostolic Church, USA, Sea Cliff, New York: Magnificent writer, a story which makes the reader become emotionally involved, a joy to read, strong Christian values. *"When God Broke Grandma's Heart"*, best seller quality.

Reverend (District Apostle Ret.) Richard C. Freund, President of The New Apostolic Church, USA. Helen's new novel, *"When God Took Grandma Home"* "Delights, brings comfort to those who grieve. Inspires, gives insight into the after-life, masterful portrayal.

Reverend Andrew Muliokela: New Apostolic Church in Alexandria, Virginia, formerly from Zambia Africa: *The Granddaughter and the Monkey Swing* and this series of books are awesome! A journey unlike another, I was reading a great novel, learning about confidence, love and support but also learning Bible verses at the same time! Helen Glowacki teaches through her books and I recommend them 100%. You'll enjoy the journey!

Reverend Frederick Rothe, (Ret. New Apostolic Church, New York) Palm Beach Gardens Congregation, Florida: Spent 48 years serving God and another 30 in the congregation. These books contain an accurate account of what God wants of us and why we suffer. The application of scripture and the people in the stories stand for the principles God wants in all of us.

Reverend Kevin Speranza, New Apostolic Church, Palm Beach Gardens, Florida: *And Then They Asked God* so happy I read this, weaves, documents biblical precepts, addresses political correctness, moral & political corruption, biased teaching, insidious growth of socialism renamed progressivism, self-importance, guilt and its debilitating power. WELL DONE! Identifies danger, artfully and Biblically addresses them.

Reverend Luke Jansen, Sr. V. P., Medical Connections, Boca Raton, Florida: "To Ms. Glowacki, author of The Grandma Series: grateful for your books, refreshing to find a Christian author who sees the *difference* between religion and spirituality AND that the two can and should be used in the same sentence.

Reverend Derryck Beukes, Montana-De Aar Congregation, Northern Cape, South Africa: Dear Helen, I personally often use your articles in my soul care visits, especially where youth are involved. I can assure you that your articles made a difference to my way of thinking, and I am busy encouraging fellow priests to read your works, as they are so factual and insightful! Thank you for your hard work. I thank God for you, and the wisdom He gave you! Please continue with the excellent work.

<u>Deacon Shadreck Wilima, Overspill Congregation, Ndola, Zambia:</u> Your articles prompt realistic examples which New Apostolic Christians need for their everyday living.

<u>Youth Chairperson, Sunday School Teacher, Mulenga Ernest, Lusaka Central Congregation, Lusaka, Zambia:</u> Through your writing I am constantly reminded of what to be aware of. I pray that God keeps you in the hollow of His hand, guards you and guides you to reach your brethren as you do me. Thanks for caring for the souls of many.

<u>Reverend Aurelio Cerullo, Atripalda Congregation in Campania, Southern Italy:</u> Dear Helen, your books and articles, and social networking bring brothers and sisters the words of our faith and touch the hearts of those who do not know our faith. Our goal isfound through the grace of the apostolate and in this sense, the word's from 1 Corinthians 15:58 assumes an important meaning: *"Therefore, my beloved brethren, be steadfast, immovable, always abounding in the work of the Lord, Knowing That your labor is not in vain in the Lord"*. Now that I am a minister of God for about a year I too am grateful to our beloved Father in Heaven for having opened the eyes of my soul, for having removed the plugs from my ears of my heart to hear and listen to His will in connection and communion with those who precede us, guided by

the light of the Holy Spirit. God's work always evolves and adapts to the times and even via computers, cell phones and smart phones. I Thank God for having been able to know you, you're a very valuable pearl. God bless you richly.

Rev. Fred Krueger, (Ret.) Lutheran Minister 12 yrs and Clinical Social Worker 26 years, Dallas, Texas: "Inspiring, grabs the heart, author headed to the bestseller list, a pleasure to read, masterful. *"When God Took Grandma Home"* filled with insight into God's plan!

NOTE: The articles which are referred to in these reviews are excerpts from Helen Glowacki's non-fiction books. Not shown are reviews by the ministers who oversee *The Henwood Foundation*'s New Apostolic Mission Schools in Zambia and review all reading materials prior to distribution.

Edith Stier, wife of a Ret. District Evangelist, Clifton, New Jersey: *The Grandma Series* helps those in need, inspirational, heartwarming, ends with a beautiful example of how God explains our pain, renews hope, shows us the way, creates miracles. I love this series.

Patricia Robinson, wife of a Ret. Rector, Indiana: 5 star rating: *When God Broke Grandma's Heart*: WONDERFUL INSPIRATIONAL NOVEL, enjoyed this book, well written, Bible references, how to achieve peace of mind and soul.

Rosemarie Schaal, wife of an Ret. Reverend, New York: *Abiding Faith, Hidden Treasure:* Reader develops empathy, feels emotion, hears a battle between scientific and spiritual knowledge. Skillful, detailed, brilliant, vivid, teaches that nothing happens that is not planned by Him.

Colette van Loggerenberg, wife of a Minister, Scottsville Congregation of Pietermaritzberg, South Africa: *Grandma's Little Book of Poetry: The Story of God's Plan of Salvation:* This has to be one of the BEST EVER books that I have read....If you ever get the chance to get one of Helen's novels...READ IT. It's like a fairytale but a TRUE fairytale.....Close your eyes and picture this: Grandma with her hair in a bun, glasses perched delicately on her nose, sitting in a rocking chair and her grandchildren sitting on the floor with BIG eyes hanging onto her every word....but with a twist!!!!! If you have doubts about PRAYER...read this book. I LOVED IT...thank you!

Debbie Espeland, wife of a Rector, Palm Beach Gardens Congregation, Florida: 5 star rating: *When God Took Grandma Home:* HEARTWARMING! This book touched my heart. It is both heartwarming and very spiritual.

Aletta Venter, wife of a Deacon, Scottsville Congregation, Pietermaritzburg, South Africa: *"Grandma's Little Book of Poetry: The Story of God's Plan of Salvation"*. What a learning process for me. Oooh I just love the way the angels are telling the story, very original! When is mankind ever going to learn? The inhabitant's lesson was to learn of good and evil. And they failed miserably each time. The devil has his agenda, and the inhabitants are the target. They call upon God for help, the angels rejoiced. Great....!!!

Aletta Venter, wife of a Deacon, Pietermaritzburg, South Africa: *"Abiding Faith, Hidden Treasure"* is the deepest and most rewarding novel I have ever read, touched my soul, made me cry, author's understanding of God's work is astounding, opens the mysteries

Lisa Mayo, wife of Minister, Palm Beach Gardens Congregation, Florida: Helen's *Why God Why* series of books gave me a new understanding of my faith. They are informative, so enlightening and in-depth, but in a way that is easily understood!!

Tammera Shelton, M.S. Psychology, Odenton, Maryland: I find *"When God Broke Grandma's Heart"* inspirational, beautifully portrays need to let go of negative events and that despite injustice, no pain is for naught.

Robert W. Rothe, USMC 1970-1976, Nevada: 5 star rating: *When God Broke Grandma's Heart:* Outstanding writer, kept me riveted, an angel sent to help through trying days. Thank you for helping me find peace.

<u>Katharina Leipp, Schopfheim, Germany</u>: This is the first time I have ever heard of a female New Apostolic author and I am very impressed by your articles. I have sent your link to my Shepherd and German friends and would like you to consider advertising in our German *Our Family Magazine.*

<u>Claudine Visagie, South Africa</u>: I'm trying to think of a way to introduce Helen's books and articles to others… especially to our youth. They are life changing!

<u>Rabecca Mukuta Mukato, Lusaka, Zambia, Africa</u>: Speaking on behalf of my Dad, District Elder Mukato, your articles are brilliant because they have changed me! Because of your articles my Dad has less headaches!

<u>Robert Henry Parkes, Pietermaritzburg, South Africa</u>: You are gifted with the verses and writings you do and are so inspiring to others. God is really using you as His special servant. You are really a wonderful person and we thank the Lord for you our sister in faith.

<u>Frank Geores, from Port St. Lucie, Florida</u>: *"When Grandma Chased The Spirits:* beautiful spiritual experience, can see caring nature and loving heart of author, eloquently reveals her love for God and search for truth. Worthy of the Star of Bethlehem rating. Thank you for sharing your magnificent gift.

Ben Lodwick, Avid Reader., from Brookfield, Wisconsin: Wow! An eye opener about God's plan of salvation, and why bad things happen to good people. Reminds me of Jim LaHaye and Jerry B. Jenkins "Left Behind Series". MUST READ!"

Dr. Walter Forman From North Palm Beach, Florida: *Grandma's Little Book of Poetry: The Story of God's Plan of Salvation:* a "wonderful book about success and failure in life. All Helen's novels are wonderful, a balm for the soul and an education to the seeker."

Susan Day, From Jupiter, Florida: *Abiding Faith, Hidden Treasure* : I hated to put it down, couldn't wait to pick it up, read all Helen's books, proves every point, shows what to do through God's words. I am 90 and Helen's books have helped me call on God.

Georgette Rothe, From Fort Piece, Florida: *Abiding Faith, Hidden Treasure* was more than I expected; a Biblical course making you re-evaluate your beliefs, enjoyed the journey very much.

Fred D'Alauro, from Palm Beach Shores, Florida: Internet 5 star rating: *When God Took Grandma Home:* Remarkable! Inspirational, moving. Fascinating storyteller with a real message.

<u>Debra Forman, Chester, New York.</u> Internet 5 star rating: *When God Broke Grandma's Heart:* Written from the heart, shares the strong beliefs that shelters us in times of need, courage captivates the reader. Thank you.

<u>Anonymous:</u> Internet 5 star rating: *When God Broke Grandma's Heart:* WHEN LIFE GETS YOU DOWN, PICK THIS BOOK UP, it wrapped its arms around me. A wonderful read. Congratulations on an inspiring work.

<u>A reviewer, a reader in Kentucky:</u> Internet 5 star rating: *When God Broke Grandma's Heart:* Well written, heartwarming, overcoming heartbreak through God, touches your heart. A worthwhile read for all generations.

<u>A reader:</u> Internet 5 star rating: *When God Broke Grandma's Heart:* a must read for all generations. FANTASTIC!

<u>A reviewer</u> Internet 5 star rating: *When God Took Grandma Home:* Moves you, captivating.

<u>A reviewer, a Kentucky reader:</u> Internet 5 star rating: *When God Took Grandma Home:* MUST READ! Touching story of life's tragedies and how lessons learned from these heartbreaking events can turn into blessings.

Description of the Characters in the Novels By Helen Glowacki

Grandma: Grandma's life was filled with sibling betrayal and marital abuse. Her love of God, home remedies and famous boxing stance touches the heart.

Sarah: Sarah helps Grandma write her journal, learns about God's plan of salvation and the enemy who wants to harm her. She carries on Grandma's legacy of faith.

Matt: Matt, Sarah's husband, has a rock-like faith but when he loses a loved one, struggles with his anger with God, until he has a miraculous experience of faith.

Paul: Paul is Matt's older brother who earned a Captain's license for a seagoing tugboat. His faith sustains him despite enduring terrible circumstances.

Mary and Kevin: Mary and Kevin become Matt and Sarah's neighbors and friends. Mary's panic attacks end when God brings a miracle they never thought possible.

Elizabeth: Elizabeth adopts Rebecca, loses her husband twelve years later, is confronted with a potentially deadly illness and searches for Rebecca's birth mother.

Rebecca: Rebecca is Elizabeth daughter and Jayden's friend. Her father's death, the illness her mother faces, and a series of challenges at college almost destroy her.

John: John, a deacon, lost his wife to a debilitating disease, becomes Elizabeth's friend, and helps his daughter and grandson through a difficult divorce.

Jayden: Jayden is John's grandson and becomes Rebecca's friend. He has learned that prayer helps solve problems and he and Rebecca begin to share their faith.

Wade and Ruth: Wade is Jim's boss and friend who adopts two children from Iraq. Ruth is Jayden's mother and John's daughter who struggles to let go of the past.

Joshua and Debbie: Joshua, Sarah's younger brother, was demanding and judgmental until Caleb stepped in. Debbie looks to Joshua's family to be her role models.

Caleb and Ann: Caleb is Sarah and Josh's older brother and the family looks to him as they once looked to Grandma. Ann, Caleb's wife harbors a secret sadness.

Barbara and Jim: Barbara, Matt's sister is also Sarah's close friend. Her husband Jim plays devil's advocate in family debates, and matchmaker for his friend Wade.

Heza and Bara: Heza and Bara endured a suicide bomber attack when Bara was one and one half years old and Heza as she was born. They are adopted by Wade.

Chaldeth: Chaldeth is a fallen angel sent to destroy Grandma's family. He plots to bring great heartache to Rebecca and Jayden and their family to break their faith.

Durk: Durk, abused by a cruel father, is a sophomore at the college Rebecca and Jayden attend. He brings harm to Rebecca and Jayden but Jim gives him a second chance.

Professsor T. Nagorra, and Emils, and Dean Peerca: These tenured professors befriend Durk and engage in activities that bring harm to the students and campus.

Professors Doog and Sendnik, and President Legna: These three share a faith in God, a love for their country, and desire to be role models. They help save the campus.

Richard and Rachel: Richard is a physician for whom Caleb built a house on the property next door to where he and Ann. live. Both couples share godly values and thus became friends.

Joe and Preacher: Both men work for the company which hired Caleb to supervise the construction of a shopping mall. Preacher is always trying to teach Joe what scripture says.

".....if ye shall hearken diligently
unto My commandments......to love
the Lord your God and to serve Him
with all your heart and with all your soul.....
I will give you the rain of your land
in his due season, the first rain and the
latter rain, that thou mayest gather in thy
corn, and thy wine, and thine oil."

Deuteronomy 11:13-14:

God's Plan of Salvation for all:

God began His plan by creating the earth in its limited universe. Then He created Adam and Eve to live happily in the Garden of Eden, walking and talking with Him. But the angel Lucifer, later known as Satan, rebelled against God because he was jealous of Christ, and of the new being, man, who God planned to elevate above the angels. (Isaiah 14:12-15) As a result of his rebellion, Satan was thrown to earth with the angels (Revelation 12:9) who followed Satan and thereby also disobeyed God. These numbered one-third of all the angels.

Satan knew God's plan and understood that when the plan was completed, and God had obtained the number of faithful loving souls He longed for, Satan would be thrown into Hell for what he had done and with him *all* evil would be forever bound. To prevent God's plan from moving forward and thus forestall his own destruction, Satan destroyed God's relationship of trust and loyalty with Adam and Eve by enticing them to sin through disobedience. Satan knew that sin would automatically separate man from God because of God's perfect righteousness.

Thus, God then had to banish Adam and Eve as he had banished Satan. (Genesis 3:1 and Genesis 3:23) But God, knowing what Satan would do, provided a way for Adam and Eve, and the generations to follow, to escape the captivity of Satan through the forgiveness of sin and return to God. In fact, this is why Christ offered Himself as the perfect sacrifice by which the sins of man could be forgiven. (John 1:29) At every turn, Satan interfered with God's plan, trying to destroy those who tried to follow God. He knew that when God collected the number of souls He desired for His new creation, Satan would be bound forever. Thus Satan is fighting for his life when trying to draw us into sin. However, because of God's love, many of those tested by Satan are strengthened through his attacks, becoming like gold refined in the fires of tribulation.

From these faithful, God is building what the Bible calls The Bride of Christ. God also provided for those who died in sin both before and after Christ provided His sacrifice by creating a means of testimony in eternity. Thus while grace is still available on earth, it is also available in eternity. Christ entered hell after His death to give testimony of His triumph to those who had died in their sins before He could bring His perfect sacrifice. (Luke 24:46) He told them that now they too could find forgiveness. (1Timothy 2:4)

A specific amount of time has been allotted in God's Plan of Salvation for His chosen ones to be made ready. (Acts 1:6-7) When that time is up, God will send His Son back to earth for the First Resurrection (Revelation 20:5) when He will take to heaven both those from eternity who have obtained forgiveness and those alive who have remained faithful. (2Peter 3:10) When they are gone, grace will also be gone, and the final destruction of the end times will begin on the earth where, among other things, one-third of all the people on earth will die. When the destruction ends, God will send His Son back to earth with those He had taken at the First Resurrection. They will have celestial (perfect) bodies, and will reign as kings and priests for one thousand years of peace to bring testimony to everyone living or dead who was not taken in the First Resurrection.

Satan will be bound during this time, unable to influence mankind, so all of mankind will learn about and accept God. But, after the one thousand years of peace, Satan will be loosed again for a little while so those who have now accepted God can be tested. (Revelation 20:7) Satan will wreak havoc on those not firm in their faith and many will leave God and follow him. (Revelation 20:2)

Then the Day of Judgment will arrive when *everyone* who was ever born, or conceived, except those taken by Christ for the First Resurrection, *will be judged.* Some of these people, which the Bible calls the "goats", will be cast into hell with Satan forever, while others, called the "lambs", will inhabit God's new kingdom where there will be no sorrow and no tears. The goats, and Satan and his angels, will be cast into the lake of fire and brimstone and tormented day and night forever. (Revelation 20:10 and 15)

Those who are taken for the First Resurrection will continue to reign as kings and priests in the new kingdom to live in the City of God. They will never have to be judged because their sins were forgiven, and entirely wiped away by God. Also important for us to know is that God wants a specific number of souls to be a part of the Bride of Christ. This is mentioned in scripture and also mentioned in the Apocrypha.

"....except that the Lord hath shortened those days, no flesh should be saved....."

Mark 13:20,

*"Receive they number O Sion,
and embrace
those of thine
that are clothed in white
which have fulfilled
the law of the Lord.
The number of thy children
whom thou longest
for, is fulfilled:
beseech the Lord that thy
people, which have been
called fromthe beginning,
may be hallowed."*

11 Esdras 2:40-41,

www.ingramcontent.com/pod-product-compliance
Lightning Source LLC
LaVergne TN
LVHW051646080426
835511LV00016B/2529